First World War
and Army of Occupation
War Diary
France, Belgium and Germany

36 DIVISION
Divisional Troops
Royal Army Veterinary Corps
48 Mobile Veterinary Section
1 October 1915 - 10 November 1919

WO95/2500/4

The Naval & Military Press Ltd
www.nmarchive.com
Published in association with The National Archives

Published by

The Naval & Military Press Ltd

Unit 10 Ridgewood Industrial Park,

Uckfield, East Sussex,

TN22 5QE England

Tel: +44 (0) 1825 749494

www.naval-military-press.com

www.nmarchive.com

This diary has been reprinted in facsimile from the original. Any imperfections are inevitably reproduced and the quality may fall short of modern type and cartographic standards.

© **Crown Copyright**
Images reproduced by permission of The National Archives, London, England, 2015.

Contents

Document type	Place/Title	Date From	Date To
Heading	WO/95/2500/4 48 Mobile Veterinary Section		
Heading	48th Mobile Vety Secn Oct 1915-Nov 1919		
Heading	30th Division 48th Mob: Vet: Sect: Vol: I		
War Diary	Bordon	01/10/1915	04/10/1915
War Diary	Southampton	05/10/1915	05/10/1915
War Diary	Havre	06/10/1915	06/10/1915
War Diary	Longeau	07/10/1915	07/10/1915
War Diary	Flesselles	08/10/1915	14/10/1915
War Diary	Ailly Sur Somme	15/10/1915	23/10/1915
War Diary	Doullens	24/10/1915	31/10/1915
Heading	36th Div 48th Mob: Vet: Sect. Vol: 2		
War Diary	Doullens	01/11/1915	27/11/1915
War Diary	L'Etoile	28/11/1915	30/11/1915
Heading	36 Div 48th Mob: Vet: Sect: Vol: 3		
War Diary	L. Etoile	01/12/1915	02/12/1915
War Diary	Bellancourt	03/12/1915	31/12/1915
Heading	48th Mob. Vet. Sect: Vol 4 Jan '16		
War Diary	Bellancourt	01/01/1916	24/01/1916
War Diary	Gorges	25/01/1916	25/01/1916
War Diary	Candas	26/01/1916	14/02/1916
War Diary	Acheux	15/02/1916	29/02/1916
Heading	48th M V S Vol 6		
War Diary	Acheux.	01/03/1916	02/04/1916
War Diary	Harponville	03/04/1916	22/06/1916
War Diary	Hedauville	23/06/1916	04/07/1916
War Diary	Toutencourt	05/07/1916	09/07/1916
War Diary	Beaumetz	10/07/1916	10/07/1916
War Diary	Auxi Le Chateau	11/07/1916	11/07/1916
War Diary	Blaringhem	12/07/1916	12/07/1916
War Diary	Tilques	13/07/1916	20/07/1916
War Diary	Ledringham	21/07/1916	21/07/1916
War Diary	Croix Rouge	22/07/1916	22/07/1916
War Diary	Ballieul	23/07/1916	31/07/1916
War Diary	B.I.D. 94 Sheet 36.	01/08/1916	17/08/1916
War Diary	S.15.c.9.7. Sheet 28.	18/08/1916	31/08/1916
War Diary	Bailleul	01/09/1916	23/03/1917
War Diary	Hoogenacker	24/03/1917	29/03/1917
War Diary	Ballieul	30/03/1917	31/03/1917
War Diary	Hoogenacker	01/04/1917	09/06/1917
War Diary	St. Jans. Cappel.	10/06/1917	24/06/1917
War Diary	Locre	25/06/1917	30/06/1917
War Diary	Merris	01/07/1917	04/07/1917
War Diary	Hondegem	05/07/1917	05/07/1917
War Diary	Arques	06/07/1917	06/07/1917
War Diary	Zudausques	07/07/1917	07/07/1917
War Diary	Acquin	08/07/1917	25/07/1917
War Diary	Noordpeene	26/07/1917	26/07/1917
War Diary	Winnizeele	27/07/1917	29/07/1917
War Diary	Watou	30/07/1917	31/07/1917
War Diary	Watou (Area)	01/08/1917	04/08/1917

War Diary	Poperinghe	05/08/1917	17/08/1917
War Diary	Winnizeele	18/08/1917	23/08/1917
War Diary	Winnizeele (Area)	24/08/1917	29/08/1917
War Diary	Etricourt	30/08/1917	30/11/1917
War Diary	Achiet-Le Petit.	01/12/1917	01/12/1917
War Diary	Beaulencourt	02/12/1917	02/12/1917
War Diary	Etricourt	03/12/1917	17/12/1917
War Diary	Courcelles	18/12/1917	18/12/1917
War Diary	Le Compte	18/12/1917	19/12/1917
War Diary	Humbercourt	19/12/1917	22/12/1917
War Diary	Mondicourt	23/12/1917	26/12/1917
War Diary	Puchevillers	27/12/1917	27/12/1917
War Diary	Corbie	28/12/1917	08/01/1918
War Diary	Harbonniere	09/01/1918	12/01/1918
War Diary	Nesle	13/01/1918	14/01/1918
War Diary	Aubigny	15/01/1918	16/01/1918
War Diary	St. Simon.	17/01/1918	28/02/1918
War Diary	Field	01/03/1918	08/03/1918
War Diary	St. Simon	09/03/1918	24/03/1918
War Diary	Field	25/03/1918	31/03/1918
War Diary	Beauchamps	01/04/1918	03/04/1918
War Diary	Field	04/04/1918	07/04/1918
War Diary	Elverdinge	08/04/1918	16/04/1918
War Diary	Proven	17/04/1918	24/04/1918
War Diary	Elverdinghe	25/04/1918	01/05/1918
War Diary	Proven	02/05/1918	02/07/1918
War Diary	Leschaeke	03/07/1918	08/07/1918
War Diary	P.34.D.1.2	09/07/1918	16/07/1918
War Diary	Sheet P.34 D.1.2.27.	17/07/1918	24/07/1918
War Diary	P.34.D.1.2.	25/07/1918	31/07/1918
War Diary	Sheet 27C P34.D.1.2	01/08/1918	25/08/1918
War Diary	P.34.D.1.2.	26/08/1918	31/08/1918
War Diary	P.34.d.1.5 Sheet 27.	01/09/1918	03/09/1918
War Diary	R 28 b 89 Sheet 27.	04/09/1918	19/09/1918
War Diary	Esquelbecq.	20/09/1918	30/09/1918
War Diary		01/10/1918	27/10/1918
War Diary	Lauwe	28/10/1918	31/10/1918
War Diary	Sterhoek	01/11/1918	01/12/1918
War Diary	Mouscron	02/12/1918	30/04/1919
War Diary	Lille	10/10/1919	10/11/1919

wo/a5/25 o/4

48 mobile Veterinary Section

36TH DIVISION
DIVL TROOPS

48TH MOBILE VETY SECN
OCT 1915 - NOV 1919

121/7517

36th Division

48th Inf. Div. Sect.
Vol: I

Oct 15
ap. '19

Army Form C. 2118.

WAR DIARY
or
INTELLIGENCE SUMMARY.
(Erase heading not required.)

Instructions regarding War Diaries and Intelligence Summaries are contained in F. S. Regs., Part II. and the Staff Manual respectively. Title pages will be prepared in manuscript.

Place	Date	Hour	Summary of Events and Information	Remarks and references to Appendices
BORDON.	1-10-15.		Routine inspection. Received G.S. wagon from A.S.C. Transfer S.S. KEW to S.V.H. BORDON. Payed men.	
"	2.10.15		Routine rifle inspection. S.S. DINSDALE taken on the strength to replace S.S. KEW.	
"	3.10.15		Routine. Stencil Pay & there Book. A.D.V.S. leaves for FRANCE	
"	4.10.15		Sleep up Camp contain at BORDON. 11·5 P.M. for SOUTHAMPTON.	
SOUTHAMPTON	5·10·15		Arrive 3 A.M. leave for HAVRE 5 P.M. on the CITY OF CHESTER.	
HAVRE	6.10.15		Arrive HAVRE 8 o'clock. proceed to REST CAMP No 5. Visits No 2. VETY HOSPITAL.	
LONGEAU	7.10.15		Arrive LONGEAU. 9·30 A.M. march to FLESSELLES. arrange billets for men & horses	
FLESSELLES.	8·10·15		Receive 8 horses for treatment. Routine rifle inspection. Rifles Ammunition & Iron Ration	
"	9.10.15		Take over charge of Units from Lt. BIDLAKE. Sent Serjeant Q Sask Transfer to A.D.V.S. Pte DUNLOP. admonished from the Charge J. Disobeying S.O. Pte RICHARDS. fined 1 day pay & extra fatigue for same thing	
"	10.10.15		Routine. D.D.V.S. visits section. Pte COUZENS. fined 2 days pay & extra fatigue for a wk. for disobeying orders	
"	11.10.15		Routine. Sent 9 sick cases to No 5 VETY HOSPITAL. ABBEVILLE	
"	12.10.15		Routine. receive mare cases for treatment. ADMS inspects villages	
"	13.10.15		Routine. Sent 15 cases to 5 VETY HOSPITAL ABBEVILLE. men parade for the purpose of being paid.	
"	14.10.15		Routine. proceed to AILLY-SUR-SOMME. to arrange billets for men & horses.	
AILLY-SUR-SOMME	15·10·15		Strike Camp. Proceed to AILLY-SUR-SOMME. this hour from AMIENS.	
"	16.10.15		Routine. Sent 20 cases to No 5 VETY HOSPITAL. ABBEVILLE	
"	17·10·15		Sent to AMIENS for float to remove horses from FLESSELLES to AILLY-SUR-SOMME (f.10) Routine.	

WAR DIARY
or
INTELLIGENCE SUMMARY.

(Erase heading not required.)

Army Form C. 2118.

Place	Date	Hour	Summary of Events and Information	Remarks and references to Appendices
AILLY SUR SOMME	18.10.15		Collect stores from ST. VAASTE. VAUX. Shot one at VILLERS BOCAGE. A.D.V.S. visits section. Routine	
"	19.10.15		Send to D.A.D.R. for remount. Dispatch 17 cases to 5 VETY. HOSPITAL. Routine. arrange for men to have a bath at M. CARMICHAELS	
"	20.10.15		Receive medicines from A.D.V.S. & distribute to V.O's in charge of units. Men paraded for being paid. Routine.	
"	21.10.15		PTE DUNLOP 11161. taken off strength & sent to A.D.V.S. Investigate outbreak of mange at BRIELLY Routine	
"	22.10.15		Send 30 cases to 5 VETY. HOSPITAL. ABBEVILLE - Routine	
"	23.10.15		Proceed to DOULLENS to arrange about billets for section	
"	24.10.15		Move from AILLY. S.U.R. SOMME where am billeted in house of MADAME BOUREZ. on DOULLENS. ALBERT. road. Routine.	
DOULLENS	25.10.15		Receive 2 cases from BIRDLAKE & 1 A.D.V.S. received 30 horses. 44 mules from 3(ONO) BASE REMOUNT DEPOT. Routine	
"	26.10.15		A.D.V.S. visits section. Remounts sent to DIV. TRAIN 2 H.D. - Routine	
"	27.10.15		Distribution of Remounts to Units. Line of front from DOULLENS Units. 1/3 LONDON R.F.A. horses in parade for pay.	
"	28.10.15		Inspect all horses of 1/3 LONDON. BDE. R.F.A. for contagious diseases also my own section. Stop same. Rortic	
"	29.10.15		Paid BOUCHIEN. VAAST. F.I.O. for hire of field. Routine.	
"	30.10.15		Routine Inspect horses 1/3 LONDON. 15DE. R.F.A. Sent 11 cases to 5 VETY HOSPITAL.	
"	31.10.15		Routine Collect horses from No.4 MOBILE VETY SECTION. also 2 Remounts from DANDAS.	

48th Indn. Petn. lett.
Vol: 2

124/7910

36th/54

WAR DIARY
or
INTELLIGENCE SUMMARY.
(Erase heading not required.)

Army Form C. 2118.

Instructions regarding War Diaries and Intelligence Summaries are contained in F.S. Regs. Part II. and the Staff Manual respectively. Title pages will be prepared in manuscript.

Place	Date	Hour	Summary of Events and Information	Remarks and references to Appendices
Doullens	1.11.15	—	Routine. Rec'd 60 REMOUNTS from DIEPPE. Distributed Same to UNITS.	
Do.	2.11.15	—	Routine. Send FLOAT. to H.P. (Qrs. 11. R.I.R. arrange for men to have 9 tail at 19 CASUALTY CLEARING STATION. A/c COUZENS attend where leave.	
Do.	3.11.15		Routine. Receive sick cases from UNITS. men paid. A/c COUZENS return	
Do.	4.11.15		Routine. Send 12. sick cases to 5. VETY HOSPITAL. ABBEVILLE.	
Do.	5.11.15		Routine. A.D.V.S. visits the section.	
Do.	6.11.15		Routine. Sold 15 sick cases to 5. VETY HOSPITAL ABBEVILLE.	
Do.	7.11.15		Routine. Purchase of CLIPPING MACHINES 51/-. Paid for hire of FLOAT. 10/-. Sold SKIN for 10/-	
Do.	8.11.15		Routine. Paid for hire of FLOAT. 10/-.	
Do.	9.11.15		Routine. Sent 26 cases to No 5 VETY HOSPITAL ABBEVILLE	
Do.	10.11.15		Routine. Rec'd from 9th R.I. Fus 27 cases for treatment. Evacuated 10 to 5 VETY HOSPITAL ABBEVILLE. Paid men. Paid for hire of FLOAT 20 frs.	
Do.	11.11.15		Routine. Sent 30 cases to No 5 VETY HOSPITAL ABBEVILLE mare for isolation	
Do.	12.11.15		Routine. 2 SUSPECTED GLANDERS	
Do.	13.11.15		Routine. Paid for hire of FLOAT. 20 frs.	
Do.	14.11.15		Routine. Sent 13 cases to 5.VETY HOSPITAL ABBEVILLE.	
Do.	15.11.15		Routine. A.D.V.S visits this section	
Do.	16.11.15		Routine. 148. Remounts arrive from DIEPPE. Distributed Same to UNITS.	
Do.	17.11.15		Routine. Sent 27 cases to No. 5 VETY HOSPITAL ABBEVILLE	
Do.	18.11.15		Routine. Paid for hire of FLOAT 50 frcs.	
Do.	19.11.15		Routine. Sent 19 cases to 5 VETY HOSPITAL ABBEVILLE	

Army Form C. 2118.

WAR DIARY
or
INTELLIGENCE SUMMARY.
(Erase heading not required.)

Instructions regarding War Diaries and Intelligence Summaries are contained in F. S. Regs., Part II. and the Staff Manual respectively. Title pages will be prepared in manuscript.

Place	Date	Hour	Summary of Events and Information	Remarks and references to Appendices
DOULLENS	20.11.15		Routine. Paid for hire of FLOAT. 15 fr.o.	
Do	21.11.15		Routine. Church Parade.	
Do	22.11.15		Routine. 8. REMOUNTS arrive from DIEPPE. Same distributed to UNITS	
Do	23.11.15		Routine. ADVS visits this section. Sent 68 cases to No 5 VETY HOSPITAL ABBEVILLE	
Do	24.11.15		Routine. Went to L'Etoile to arrange Billets for men + horses.	
Do	25.11.15		Routine. DDVS visits this section. Paid men	
Do	26.11.15		Routine. Sent 18 cases to 5 VTY HOSPITAL ABBEVILLE	
Do	27.11.15		Routine. Sent 9 cases to Do Do	
L'Etoile	28.11.15		Section moves to L'Etoile.	
Do	29.11.15		Routine. Received 87 REMOUNTS. Same distributed to UNITS. ADVS visits section	
Do	30.11.15		Routine. Distribute remainder of REMOUNTS to UNITS	

48th Indi. Feb. Sess.
Vol. 3

121/7910

3655-

Army Form C. 2118.

WAR DIARY
or
INTELLIGENCE SUMMARY.
(Erase heading not required.)

Instructions regarding War Diaries and Intelligence Summaries are contained in F.S. Regs., Part II. and the Staff Manual respectively. Title pages will be prepared in manuscript.

Place	Date	Hour	Summary of Events and Information	Remarks and references to Appendices
L. ETOILE	1.12.15		Routine. Section proceeds to BELLANCOURT to arrange billets for men & horses.	
do	2.12.15		SECTION proceeds to BELLANCOURT	
BELLANCOURT	3.12.15		Routine. Sent 36 sick ones to No 14 VETy. HP ABBEVILLE. Paid men	
do	4.12.15		Routine saddle inspection	
do	5.12.15		Routine. Sent 14 sick cases to 14 Vty. H.P. ABBEVILLE. ADVS visits this section. 2 Glanders horses isolated with a negative result.	
do	6.12.15		Routine examined scrapings of 3 Mange cases with a negative result.	
do	7.12.15		Routine proceed to PONT REMY. for post mortem on horse.	
do	8.12.15		Routine. Sent 13 sick cases to 14 Vty HP. ABBEVILLE	
do	9.12.15		Routine. Proceed to 14 Vty HP ABBEVILLE arranges about fresh, 4 SUS GLANDERS. arrive from 1/2 LONDON for isolation	
do	10.12.15		Routine Paid men. 2 men taken in strength from No 2 VTY HP HAVRE 1 SUS GLANDERS arrive from 1/2 LONDON for isolation	
do	11.12.15		Routine. Sent 18 cases for further treatment to 14 VTY HP ABBEVILLE	
do	12.12.15		Routine. Took over 25 SUS MANGE Cases from 10 DAC. CAPT. CONNYOCHIE. & BATMAN taken on strength temporary	
do	13.12.15		Routine sent 28 Cases to 14 VTY HOSPITAL ABBEVILLE	
do	15.12.15		Routine. Took over. 57 unsounds. + paired Same to UNITS.	
do	14.12.15		Routine. clothing + KIT inspection	
do	16.12.15		Routine sent 11 Cases for treatment to 14 VTY HOSP. ABBEVILLE	

WAR DIARY
or
INTELLIGENCE SUMMARY.

(Erase heading not required.)

Army Form C. 2118.

Place	Date	Hour	Summary of Events and Information	Remarks and references to Appendices
BELLANCOURT	17.12.15		Routine ADVS visits section for purpose of ensuring remounts distributed to units BDR visits section of ensuring horses. Paid men.	
Do	18.12.15		Routine Pte DINSDALE absent without leave after 8.30 P.M. 1 Sus GLANDERS await for rotation from 173 BDE. RFA.	
Do	19.12.15		Routine Pte Read asleep on his post.	
Do	20.12.15		Routine ADVS visits section sent 43 cases to 14 VTY HP ABBEVILLE	
Do	21.12.15		Routine. Malleined 36 animals of 9 R.I.F. 9th Fus. 41 of 121 Bde. bay. R.E. 10 of MOBILE VETY SECTION 48th
Do	22.12.15		Routine Examined malleined Remounts A.D.V.S visits section
Do	23.12.15		Routine malleined remaining animals of 9 R.I.F. 121 FLD COY RE + MOBILE SECTION Inspected 108 BDE UNITS. 7 cock cases to 14 VTY HP ABBEVILLE
Do	24.12.15		Routine Examined malleined animals 9 R.I.F. 1st FIELD COY R.E. M.V.S. drew 1000 feed from FIELD CASHIER Inspected 12 BDE units, Drew 9 Remounts from ABBEVILLE SUS GLANDER sent for isolation from 172 BDE RFA.
Do	25.12.15		Routine. Examined malleined horses of above UNITS. Malleined ADVS visits section
Do	26.12.15		Routine. Paid men. Holds horse for GLANDERS.
Do	27.12.15		Routine. 9 cases to VTY HP No 14 ABBEVILLE.
Do	28.12.15		Routine ADVS + DDVS visits section for post mortem on GLANDERED horse. MEDICAL Inspection 108 BDE Inspected animals of 2 Boy ASC + 2nd Batt 3 LANCS.
Do	29.12.15		Routine Inspected malleined animals 9 108 BDE malleined horses 9 121 FLD COY RE
Do	30.12.15		Routine Paid men. took over 83 REMOUNTS & distributed same to units TESTED 5 GLANDERS SUS. from Y/ LONDON
Do	31.12.15		Routine sent 33 cases to 14 VTY HP ABBEVILLE	

Ltr Ind. rev Secr.
vol 4
Jan '16

36

Army Form C. 2118.

WAR DIARY
or
INTELLIGENCE SUMMARY.
(Erase heading not required.)

Instructions regarding War Diaries and Intelligence Summaries are contained in F.S. Regs., Part II. and the Staff Manual respectively. Title pages will be prepared in manuscript.

Place	Date	Hour	Summary of Events and Information	Remarks and references to Appendices
BELLANCOURT	1.1.16		Routine. Despatch. 83 sick cases to 14. VETY. HOSP. 6 unspecial GLANDERS admitted	
do	2.1.16		Routine. Despatch 24 sick cases. To 22 VETY. HOS.. Decline to 22 VTY. Officers on a. MOBILE VETY. SECTION. Destroy 2. mules to mallein test belonging to 2/2 LONDON. BDE. make a POSTMORTEM on same. DDVS + ADVS present. Proceed to CANAPLES to arrange billets for men + horses. N°. H14. Pte SQUIRES taken on the strength from N°. 6 VETY. I.P. I.P. Reactor to mallein test arrives for isolation from 154th BDE:-	
do	3.1.16		Routine. SERGT. JAMES. 712 proceeds on leave. till 11.1.16. N°102248. PTE COUZENS. G.E transferred To N° 6 VETY HOS. Report 4 ADVS on Glanders cases. Despatch 21 cases to 32 VET HOS. Handed out to ADVANCED TRANSPORT. DEPÔT. I.G.S. LIMB WAGGON. in exchange for 1. HORSE FLOAT.	
do	4.1.16		Routine. 1. P. reactor to mallein test arrives for isolation.	
do	5.1.16		Routine. Receive 1 G.S LIMB wagon. from A.T DEPOT.	
do	6.1.16		Routine. Despatch 14 cases To 22 VTY. HOSP.	
do	7.1.16		Routine. 1 reactor to mallein test arrive from 1/5 10TH LANCS. to be isolated. INTRA INTER-PALPEBRAL same date. A.D.V.S. took action.	
do	8.1.16		Routine. PTE COUZENS. 10248. averts from NO. 6. VETY. HOSP. & arrests at 4 &7th M.V.S	
do	9.1.16		Routine. 2.P reactors of the 173rd BDE tested INTER PALPEBRALLY. Despatch 19 cases to 22 VET. I.P.	
do	10.1.16		Routine. 2.P. reactor of the 173 Bde tested SUBCUTANEOUSLY. 2. Pauline reactors arrive from DIV.SIG. COY + DIV CAV. negatively to be isolated, STERN + MORRIS Evacuated with GERMAN MEASLES. to hospital.	
do	12.1.16		Routine. 2 : 173rd BDE horse. Phew & negative mallein react. to testing. SERGT. JAMES. return.	

Army Form C. 2118.

WAR DIARY
or
INTELLIGENCE SUMMARY.
(Erase heading not required.)

Instructions regarding War Diaries and Intelligence Summaries are contained in F.S. Regs., Part II. and the Staff Manual respectively. Title pages will be prepared in manuscript.

Place	Date	Hour	Summary of Events and Information	Remarks and references to Appendices
BELLANCOURT	11.1.16.		Routine. Despatch 24 cases to 22 VETY. HOSP. Proceed to ABBEVILLE for the purpose of seeing D.V.S. Pte COUZENS. 10248. SENT by escort to No. 5. VETY. H.P.	
do	13.1.16.		Routine. Take over & distribute 155 Remounts to UNITS.	
do	14.1.16.		Routine. Report to ADVS on 173RD BDE horses. distribute remaining remounts to UNITS.	
do	15.1.16.		Routine. admitted 12 MANGE cases from 4th WEST. LANCS. HOW BDE. RFA.	
do	16.1.16.		Routine. despatch 29 cases to 22 VET. HOS. PAID men. 1 Periodical Reactor. arrive for vacation from 122 FIELD COY. R.E.	
do	17.1.16.		Routine. despatch 22 sick cases to No. 22. VETY HOSP.	
do	18.1.16.		Routine. despatched 3 cases to No 22 VETY HOSP for fomit.	
do	19.1.16.		Routine. A.D.V.S visits section	
do	20.1.16.		Routine. despatch 15 cases to 22 YETY HOS.	
do	21.1.16.		Routine. Ystid INTER. PALPEBRAL 3 horses 1/2 LONDON BDE. - 4 horses 154TH BDE. 3 horses. - 36TH UDAC. 1 horse - 153RD BDE.	
do	22.1.16.		Routine. tested above cases SUBCUTANEOUSLY. dispatched 16 cases to 22 VETY. HOS.	
do	23.1.16.		Routine 14 can despatched to No 22 VETY HOS.	
do	24.1.16.		Routine. despatched 2 cases to 22 VETY. HOS. for fomit. Pat martin in 1 horse. 36 UDAC. 1 horse 154 BDE. listed with a positive result. ADVS present.	
GORGES	25.1.16.		SECTION. proceed to GORGES.	
CANDAS	26.1.16.		SECTION. proceed to CANDAS. ADVS visits section	
do	27.1.16.		Routine. admitted 3 mange cases from 36. UDAC.	
do				

Army Form C. 2118.

WAR DIARY
or
INTELLIGENCE SUMMARY.
(Erase heading not required.)

Instructions regarding War Diaries and Intelligence Summaries are contained in F.S. Regs., Part II, and the Staff Manual respectively. Title pages will be prepared in manuscript.

Place	Date	Hour	Summary of Events and Information	Remarks and references to Appendices
CANDAS.	28.1.16		Routine Visits & Statistical ?? Remarks. 20 UNITS. DDVR.&D.VS. present. AA.QMG. paid a visit. Total 2 horses 1 from 18 R.I.R. + 1 from 1/5 5TH LANCS. INTER. PALPEBRALLY.	
do	29.1.16		Routine. Treated above horse SUBCUTANEOUSLY. Inoculated 37 horses & 22 VET HOSP.	
do	30.1.16		Routine. 2 horses above show a negative result to Malein Paire ???.	
do	31.1.16		Routine. Tested INTER. PALPEBRALLY. 1 horse - 36. DIV. SIG. COY. 1 horse - 122. FIELD. COY. R.E. 1 horse . DIV. CAVLRY.	

WAR DIARY or INTELLIGENCE SUMMARY

Army Form C. 2118

Place	Date	Hour	Summary of Events and Information	Remarks and references to Appendices
CANDAS.	1.2.16		Routine. Sent 30 cases to No. 22 VETY. HOSPITAL. proceed to DOULLENS vie BILLS.	
do	2.2.16		Coked 3 remaining horses. Subcutaneously 122 FIELD COY. RE. 36 DIVL SIG COY. & 6TH ENNIS. DRAGS. respectively. Pte. BURRELL & READ return from leave. Pte. FITZPATRICK granted leave. A.D.V.S visits section to inspect mallender horses & mule.	
do	3.2.16		Routine. Sent 43 cases to 22. VET. HOS. view surplus horses. Report on glanders to A.D.V.S.	
do	4.2.16		Routine. A.D.V.S. inspects glander cases. admitted 2 Sno mange from 36. U.D.A.C.	
do	5.2.16		Routine. Sent to LONGUEVILLERS for 10 sick knee pains men. destroy mule from 122 FIELD. COY. RE. Post mortin in above reveals organ normal. ADVS present	
do	6.2.16		Routine. Proceed to DOULLENS. 5AM. to view 29. remounts to 108. BDE. 109. BDE + 12. BDE. Pte. EVANS 5699 taken on strength from 12. MOB. VT. SECT. TUBE HELMET. issue for section.	
do	7.2.16		Routine. sent 23 cases to 22. VET. HOS. Report on mange cases UDAC + 1/ CHES to A.D.V.S.	
do	8.2.16		Routine. issue 8 horses. to 108. BDE. PTE. FARLEY returns from leave. have over 11 cases to 55 MOB. VETY. SECT.	
do	9.2.16		Section move to ACHEUX. 29 remounts collected from DOULLENS.	
do	10.2.16		Routine. pour remounts to DIVNL. UNITS. SERGT. BIGNALL proceeds on leave.	
do	11.2.16		Routine. Paid men. Pte. STERN + MORRIS struck of strength permanently + taken on strength of No. 6 VET. HOS	
do	12.2.16		Routine. PTE. FITZPATRICK returns from leave	
do	13.2.16		Routine. sent 21 cases to 22 VET. HOS. front train to MESNIL	
do	14.2.16		Routine. PTE. EVANS + GORDON. granted leave.	

Army Form C. 2118

WAR DIARY
or
INTELLIGENCE SUMMARY
(Erase heading not required.)

Instructions regarding War Diaries and Intelligence Summaries are contained in F. S. Regs., Part II. and the Staff Manual respectively. Title Pages will be prepared in manuscript.

Place	Date	Hour	Summary of Events and Information	Remarks and references to Appendices
ACHEUX	15.2.16		Routine. Outbreak of Mange in 127 BDE RFA. All horses in Brigade Isolated & dressed. PTE. BARRATT returns from leave.	
do	16.2.16		Routine. Ordain fatigue party from INNIS. FUS. for the purpose of building standing for sick horses.	
do	17.2.16		Routine. Above fatigue party still employed as above.	
do	18.2.16		Routine. Inspected Animals of 127 BDE, RFA.	
do	19.2.16		Routine. Paid men. SERGT SCHOLFIELD & LCPL MACCAMMON granted leave.	
do	20.2.16		Routine. 2 mules sent to Euves to 22 VET HOS.	
do	21.2.16		Routine. distilled Remounts at LONGPRÉ STATION. 127 BDE animals dressed with CALC. SULPHIDE	
do	22.2.16		Routine. dispensed with fatigue party's services.	
do	23.2.16		Routine. Stables disinfected of 127 BDE. RFA.	
do	24.2.16		Routine. 18 cases to 22 VET. HOS. PTE. EVANS returns from leave.	
do	25.2.16		Routine. Paid men. THAW emergency orders in force. Sent 1 GS WAGON, & 2 men to SUPPLY COLUMN. Received horse from 6TH ENNIS DRAGS for men attached. PTE GORDON returns from leave.	
do	26.2.16		Routine. Distributed Remounts at DOULLENS brought 6 to section.	
do	27.2.16		Routine. Issued mite from 36 DDAC & more from DIV. SIG. COY. RE interpolatorly. Inspected mange cases 127 BDE with ADVS. Result of testing Mageum.	
do	28.2.16		Routine. Scrapings taken mange cases from 109 INF. BDE. Give a positive microscopic result.	
do	29.2.16		Routine. SERGT SCHOLFIELD & LCPL MACCAMMON return from leave. Despatch 16 cases to 22 VET. HOS.	A Chown Cpt B.C.

48ª MVS
Vol 6

WAR DIARY
or
INTELLIGENCE SUMMARY

(Erase heading not required.)

Army Form C. 2118

Instructions regarding War Diaries and Intelligence Summaries are contained in F.S. Regs., Part II. and the Staff Manual respectively. Title Pages will be prepared in manuscript.

Place	Date	Hour	Summary of Events and Information	Remarks and references to Appendices
ACHEUX	1.3.16		Routine. 2 Glanders cases returned from isolation.	
do	2.3.16		Routine. Paid men.	
do	3.3.16		Routine. Obtain fatigue party from Town Commandant for the purpose of building stunnings.	
do	4.3.16		Routine. Despatched 22 sick cases to No. 22 VETY HOSPITAL	
do	5.3.16		Routine. D.D.V.S. 4TH ARMY & A.D.V.S. visits section	
do	6.3.16		Routine. Injected horse from 154 BDE. RFA with ANTI TETANUS SERUM.	
do	7.3.16		Routine. Exercised 2 mules from VAL DE MAISON.	
do	8.3.16		Routine. Despatched horse to No. 22 VETY 1-10S. belonging to 36 D.A.C. admitted. 1 suspected MANGE from 154 BDE. RFA.	
do	9.3.16		Routine. Left P.M. on horse inoculated with Shrapnel in shoulder. Report to A.D.V.S. same eve.	In/3/16 1.4.16
do	10.3.16		Routine. A.D.V.S. visits section	
do	11.3.16		Routine. Imperial at F.G.C.M. on 721 SERGT FANE.J.B.K. of this section charged with drunkenness. O.A.S.	
do	12.3.16		Routine. Took over T Chalebled Remounts at DOULLENS.	
do	13.3.16		Routine. Distributed remainder of Remounts to units.	
do	14.3.16		Routine. Issued surplus remounts to units.	
do	15.3.16		Routine. Sentence on 721 SERGT FANE promulgated. Reduced to rank of Cpl. Despatched 10 cases to No. 22 VET. HOS.	
do	16.3.16		Routine. A.D.V.S visits section.	
do	17.3.16		Routine. Paid men. Admitted one suspected MANGE case from 153rd BDE.	

WAR DIARY
or
INTELLIGENCE SUMMARY
(Erase heading not required.)

Army Form C. 2118

Instructions regarding War Diaries and Intelligence Summaries are contained in F. S. Regs., Part II. and the Staff Manual respectively. Title Pages will be prepared in manuscript.

Place	Date	Hour	Summary of Events and Information	Remarks and references to Appendices
ACHEUX.	18.3.16		Routine. Report on MANGE cases to A.D.V.S.	
do	19.3.16		Routine. Admitted one MANGE case from 8 R.I.R. report to ADVS on same	
do	20.3.16		Routine. Allain fatigue party & GS wagon for making plankings	
do	21.3.16		Routine. CAPT CHOWN. Granvick leaves. CAPT McCLINTOCK who charge of 48 M.V.S	
do	22.3.16		Routine. D.D.V.S 4th Army + ADVS visits section	
do	23.3.16		Routine. PTE GORDON evacuated from 110 FIELD AMBULANCE - Paris new - ADVS & OC 48 M.V.S disinfect 69 remounts at BELLE ÉGLISE	
do	24.3.16		Routine. Despatch 26 cases to 22 VET. HOS.	
do	25.3.16		Routine. PTE RICHARDS.11062 proceeds to WAR OFFICE pursuant to taking of a conversion. Admit 2 MANGE cases from 153 BDE macroscopic examination of 1 Suspected MANGE case from 153 BDE negative. Report sent to ADVS	
do	26.3.16		Routine. 721 CPL. FANE. transferred to N°. 3 VET. HOS.	
do	27.3.16		Routine. A.D.M.S visits section	
do	28.3.16			
do	29.3.16		Routine. B.D.R 4th ARMY + ADVS visits section for cooking horses.	
do	30.3.16		Routine. Paris new.	
do	31.3.16		Routine. CAPT. CHOWN returns from leave.	

48.M.V.S.
Vol 7

Army Form C. 2118

WAR DIARY
or
INTELLIGENCE SUMMARY
(Erase heading not required.)

Instructions regarding War Diaries and Intelligence Summaries are contained in F. S. Regs., Part II. and the Staff Manual respectively. Title Pages will be prepared in manuscript.

Place	Date	Hour	Summary of Events and Information	Remarks and references to Appendices
ACHEUX	1.4.16		Routine – Rifle inspection. Take over GENERALS horse for treatment	
do	2.4.16		Routine – mule admitted from 8 R.I.R. with SUS. MANGE. despatch 26. cases to No. 22 VETY HOSPITAL	
HARPONVILLE	3.4.16		Routine – Section proceeds to HARPONVILLE	
do	4.4.16		Routine. took over from A.D.V.S. D.H.Q units & 172 BDE.	
do	5.4.16		Routine. A.D.M.S. visits section. Sent in returns for Medicine	
do	6.4.16		Routine – Paid men. Visit & inspect horses of 172 BDE. R.F.A. Rifle inspection	
do	7.4.16		Routine. Went to MESNIL. despatch 20 cases to No. 22 VET. HOS	
do	8.4.16		Routine – look over & disinfect 7 Remounts 16 36 DIVNL UNITS.	
do	9.4.16		Routine. horses belonging to 153 BDE R.F.A. PM on dead horse belonging to 172 BDE RFA. Analysis forwarded to Remounts.	
do	10.4.16		Routine – D.D.R. visits section for the purpose of casting horses. Men under orders for 15 Ordnance. Rifle inspection	
do	11.4.16		Routine – despatch 22 cases to No 22 VETY HOS	
do	12.4.16		Routine. admit 16 DEBILITY cases from 153 BDE.	
do	13.4.16		Routine. Retrieve 2nd horse Rugs & 2nd Brushes & to ORDNANCE	

Army Form C. 2118

WAR DIARY
or
INTELLIGENCE SUMMARY
(Erase heading not required.)

Place	Date	Hour	Summary of Events and Information	Remarks and references to Appendices
HARPONVILLE	14.4.16		Routine despatch 30 cases to No. 22 VETY HOS.	
do	15.4.16		Routine. D.D.V.S. visits & inspects section, inspect D Batty. 178 BDE	
do	16.4.16		Routine. Section publication in BVNL ORDERS, for having extremely well kept lines	
do	17.4.16		Routine despatched 28 cases to No. 22 VETY HOS. Visit to 173 BDE with A.D.V.S.	
do	18.4.16		Routine. Inspect HEAD QRS. animals & attached Rifles inspection	
do	19.4.16		Routine PM on BRN.G. - 173 BDE A.C. received 5 gals LINSEED OIL 15 C/By 173 BDE	
do	20.4.16		Routine. took over & distributed 100 Remounts from DIEPPE	
do	21.4.16		Routine. Proceed to AMIENS to purchase Sayer Sioux. distayed (porohn heg). by DIV. CAVALRY.	
do	22.4.16		Routine. Chest Charger belonging 16 CAPT COOTE ponka leg drainaged	
do	23.4.16		Routine ADVS into action, despatched 32 cases 16 22 VETY HOS.	
do	24.4.16		Routine visit & inspect 15 H B.R.C.	
do	25.4.16		Routine Saddler inspection. took over duties of TOWN MAJOR HARPONVILLE	

Army Form C. 2118

WAR DIARY
or
INTELLIGENCE SUMMARY
(Erase heading not required.)

Instructions regarding War Diaries and Intelligence Summaries are contained in F. S. Regs., Part II. and the Staff Manual respectively. Title Pages will be prepared in manuscript.

Place	Date	Hour	Summary of Events and Information	Remarks and references to Appendices
HARPONVILLE	26.4.16		Routine. Drew 1000 Frcs from FIELD CASHIER. Paid men	
do	27.4.16		Routine. Received 3 Remounts from BELLE EGLISE also 3 Chargers for VIII CORPS.	
do	28.4.16		Routine. distributed. 7 Reviews 15 DIV CAVALRY. PUCHEVILLERS	
do	29.4.16		Routine. visited 107 BDE. H.Q. 2Rs. also 154 B.A.C distributed Chargers to 107 MACHINE GUN Co. + C Batty 173 BDE.	
do	30.4.16		Routine. Church Parade for all Ranks C.E.	

Army Form C. 2118

WAR DIARY
or
INTELLIGENCE SUMMARY
(Erase heading not required.)

4 8 Font Vet... *Vol 8* *XXXVI*

Instructions regarding War Diaries and Intelligence Summaries are contained in F.S. Regs., Part II. and the Staff Manual respectively. Title Pages will be prepared in manuscript.

Place	Date	Hour	Summary of Events and Information	Remarks and references to Appendices
Harponville	1-5-16		Routine. Despatched 30 Sick Cases to H.Q. 22 Veterinary Hospital.	
	2-5-16		Routine. Admitted horse from D Batt'y. 154th Bde R.A. with Jaundice. Ireland to go clothing for Section.	
	3-5-16		Pte No. 11090. G. Osborne proceeds on leave for 8 days. — Routine — Pte No. 414 C. Lyons transferred to H.Q. 2 Veterinary Hospital. Collected 2 A.D. from 48 Division at BERTRANCOURT CHURCH. Repaired & A.D.V.S. re dumping of Shoes in case of a move.	
	4-5-16		Routine. Took over 69 remounts at RAILHEAD and distributed Same. A.D.V.S. visits Section.	
	5-5-16		Routine. Issue remounting remounts. Paid men.	
	6-5-16		Routine. Pte. No. 11616 R. Gibson proceeds on 8 days leave. Inspect animals at TOUTENCOURT	
	7-5-16		Routine. Visited and Inspected 109th Inf Bde. HQ 2nd Armoured 154th Bde.	
	8-5-16		Flour proceed to MARTINSART for mutual Shrapnel wounds. Ireland for drugs. Routine. Pte No. T.3/031088 M. Young transferred to H.Q. 1 Coy A.S.C. H.Q. T.4/056144. Pte J. Bramhall transferred from No. 1 Coy A.S.C.	
	9-5-16		Evacuated 12 cases to No. 22 Veterinary Hospital. Routine. Drew 1000 forms from Field Cashier.	
	10-5-16		Routine. Admitted 1 Suspected Mange case from A Bett'y 153rd Bde. R.A.	
	11-5-16		Routine. Inspected 172nd Bde R.A. at TOUTENCOURT and 154th Bde. Amm Column.	

Army Form C. 2118

WAR DIARY
or
INTELLIGENCE SUMMARY
(Erase heading not required.)

Instructions regarding War Diaries and Intelligence Summaries are contained in F. S. Regs., Part II. and the Staff Manual respectively. Title Pages will be prepared in manuscript.

Place	Date	Hour	Summary of Events and Information	Remarks and references to Appendices
HARPONVILLE	12.5.16		No. 11090 Pte Osborne. J. return from leave of absence. Evacuated 17 cases to J.O. 22 Veterinary Hospital	
	13.5.16		ABBEVILLE. Routine.	
	14.5.16		Routine. Animals for casting at Section inspected by D.D.V. Paid men.	
			A.D.V.S. visits Section. Issued flour to M2 Bde R.F.A. Church Parade. Routine.	
	15.5.16		Routine. Visited Gas Inspected 109th Bde. Hd Qs. 154th Bde from CO2 and 172 V Bge R.F.A.	
	16.5.16		Routine. Sere new Veterinary Charge of B ECHELON at HARPONVILLE. J°. 11432 Corporal	
			Brier. R.V. Gust J°. 11339 C Ireland. J.A. granted 8 days leave.	
	17.5.16		Evacuated 64 cases to J.O. 22 Veterinary Hospital. Routine.	
	18.5.16		Routine. Collected 17 HD horses from 29 D.A.C. Visit and Inspect 173rd Bde horses	
			at TOUTENCOURT.	
	19.5.16		Routine. Inspecting horse collected from D.A.C.	
	20.5.16		Routine. Drew 100 feet from Field Canteen. Pas hoes Evacuated 22 cases to	
			Veterinary Hospital	
	21.5.16		Routine. Issue proceed to PUCHEVILLERS. Inspect 173 Bge. B Echelon 4 109th Bde. Ad Qs.	

Army Form C. 2118

WAR DIARY
or
INTELLIGENCE SUMMARY
(Erase heading not required.)

Instructions regarding War Diaries and Intelligence Summaries are contained in F.S. Regs., Part II. and the Staff Manual respectively. Title Pages will be prepared in manuscript.

Place	Date	Hour	Summary of Events and Information	Remarks and references to Appendices
HARPONVILLE	22.5.16		Routine. Received 1 suspected mange case from No. 1 Coy A.S.C.	
	23.5.16		Reported on suspected mange case. Visit 172 Bde R.F.A. horses.	
	24.5.16		Evacuated 28 cases to ABBEVILLE. Inspected horses of B. ECHELON. 36 D.A.C.	
	25.5.16		Visited and inspected 172 Bde animals at TOUTENCOURT. Routine.	
	26.5.16		Evacuated 22 cases to No. 22 Hospital. Corporal No. 11432 J.R. Buck and Dr. No. 11339	
	27.5.16		J.H. Ireland returned from leave of absence. Routine.	
			Routine. A.D.V.S. Visited Section. Inspected B. Echelon. Paid men.	
	28.5.16		Routine. Received 7 horses from B.A.C. details.	
	29.5.16		Routine. Pt. No. 3312. L. Cohen. Pt. No. 2484. K.F. Brickett and Dr. No. 11519 J. Warner were given extra Guards on fatigues for 2 weeks for having dirty Rifles.	
	30.5.16		Routine. Inspected horses at TOUTENCOURT.	
	31.5.16		Routine. No. 8702. Sergt. F. M. Sampson, taken on the strength of the Section. A.D.V.S. Visits the Section. Routine. Visited horses at TOUTENCOURT.	

48. M. Vet. Sec
Army Form C. 2118
Vol 9 June

WAR DIARY or INTELLIGENCE SUMMARY

(Erase heading not required.)

Instructions regarding War Diaries and Intelligence Summaries are contained in F.S. Regs., Part II. and the Staff Manual respectively. Title Pages will be prepared in manuscript.

No. MV 3/86
Date 1.7.16

Place	Date	Hour	Summary of Events and Information	Remarks and references to Appendices
HARPONVILLE	1.6.16		Routine take over 32 Remounts from RAILHEAD. 24 animals evacuated to No 22 VETY. HOSPITAL.	
"	2.6.16		Routine. Visit & inspect B. ECHELON DAC., HQ 2RS, 10g. INF. BDE. Weekly return to ADVS. Paid men.	
"	3.6.16		Routine Distributed Remounts to Units of 36 DIVN. Visit 172 BDE. at TOUTENCOURT. Make contract with S'VAASTE DOULLENS' for purchase of unserviceable horses.	
"	4.6.16		Routine. Church parade for men. Send 1 set of PM instruments to ADVS 49 DIVN. Dispose of unserviceable horses to S' VAASTE. BOUCHERIE. DOULLENS for 150 frans.	
"	5.6.16		Routine dispose of unserviceable horse to Vaast. BOUCHERIE DOULLENS for 150 frs ADVS visits section. Inspect 11 + 13 R.I.R. N° 5699 Pte EVANS GE confined to Barracks for 14 days for Conduct respect to prepare	
"	6.6.16		Routine. Hospital 21 cases to No 22 VETY HOSPITAL, Visit B'ECHELON DAC 1 Case of GLANDERS reported from 173 BDE. Dr BRACE remained for Court Martial	
"	7.6.16		Routine Inspects 172 BDE RFA with ADVS.	
"	8.6.16		Routine ADVS visits section. Party men receive a les MANGE case from A BATTY 153 BDE inspect "B" ECHELON DAC.	
"	9.6.16		Routine. forward summary of evidence concerning DR BRACE. A.S.C. to ADVS.	

WAR DIARY or INTELLIGENCE SUMMARY

Army Form C. 2118

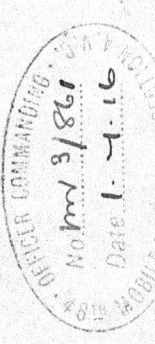

Place	Date	Hour	Summary of Events and Information	Remarks and references to Appendices
HARPONVILLE	10.6.16		Routine. visited 173 BDE at TOUTENCOURT. reported on SUS MANGE case. A. BATTY 153 BDE	
	11.6.16		Routine. positive result of microscopic examination of 153 BDE MANGE case.	
	12.6.16		Routine. A.D.V.S. visit section. deputated 2D Sick animals to No 7 VETY HOSPITAL. return Col PLAICE's charger. Report to A.D.V.S. re FEVER case in unit.	
	13.6.16		Routine. Prosecute in COURT MARTIAL on T3/031306 DR BRACE. A.S.C. Section again in DIVL ORDERS for having as prisoners under kept billets	
	14.6.16		Routine. visit 11th & 13th R.I.R. Pay to 313 PTE COHEN. 250 FRCS. attend conference at A.D.V.S. office. his time expired. 11 P.M. clocks advanced 1 hour.	
	15.6.16		Routine. Pte COHEN proceeds on 8 days leave. commencing 15th. Dispose of three unserviceable horses to L. VAASTE. DOULLENS. for 450 FRCS. Iche Helmet inspection	
	16.6.16		Routine. take over & distribute 49 Remounts. at Rackeau. visit section	
	17.6.16		Routine. dispatch 35 cases to No 7 VETY HOSPITAL. visit ADVANCED VETY AID POST. with ADVS.	

Army Form C. 2118

WAR DIARY
or
INTELLIGENCE SUMMARY
(Erase heading not required.)

Instructions regarding War Diaries and Intelligence Summaries are contained in F.S. Regs., Part II. and the Staff Manual respectively. Title Pages will be prepared in manuscript.

Place	Date	Hour	Summary of Events and Information	Remarks and references to Appendices
HARPONVILLE	18.6.16		Routine. No 8702 Pte SAMPSON P.V.M. transferred to No 2 VETY HOSPITAL. Draw 1000 frs from FIELD CASHIER.	
"	19.6.16		Routine. Vet ADVS at HEDAUVILLE. Take helmet inspection.	
"	20.6.16		Routine. Receive on SUS MANGE case from 466 Coy ASC. Receive 10 men from No 2nd VETY HOSPITAL for evacuating sick & wounded horses. Vaast SVAASTE & dispose by HIDES.	
"	21.6.16		Routine. Dispatch 18 sick animals to No 7 VETY HOSPITAL.	
"	22.6.16		Routine. Paid men. ADVS visits section under orders to move to HEDAUVILLE.	
HEDAUVILLE	23.6.16		Move to HEDAUVILLE. Take over charge of all units in HEDAUVILLE employed. 7 men with sick animals of 32 DIVN. Routine. Put on ADVANCED VETY AID POST.	
"	24.6.16			
"	25.6.16		Routine. Dispatch 20 sick animals to No 7 VETY HOS. Take over GEN HICKMANS charger.	
"	26.6.16		Routine. Take over & distribute 6.5 Remounts, admit SUS MANGE case from 135 FLD Coy RE	
"	27.6.16		Routine. Dispatch 3 men with sick animals of 32 DIVN.	
"	28.6.16		Routine. Despatch 18 sick animals to No 7 VETY HOS. Despatch 3 men with animals of 32 DIV.	
"	29.6.16		Routine. Take over 16 Remounts for 20 Regiment D'ARTILLERIE. GROUP DE VARINE. Pte OSBORNE & Pte EVANS awarded 14 Days FP No 1 for being absent at ROMES CAMP while carrying out horses parade.	
"	30.6.16		Routine. Take over 6 sick animals from FRENCH ARTILLERIE	

WAR DIARY or INTELLIGENCE SUMMARY

Army Form C. 2118

36 July
48th Mot. Vet. Sec.
Vol 10

Place	Date	Hour	Summary of Events and Information	Remarks and references to Appendices
HEDAUVILLE	1.7.16		Routine. despatch 23 cases to No 7 VETY HOSPITAL. Take over Remounts at QUERRIEUX	
do	2.7.16		Routine. Take over 63 Remounts from RAILHEAD. & dislocheli 16 think - Send horse. to DOULLENS & dispose of for 150 FRCS to L VAASTE	
do	3.7.16		Routine. Send 2 men to 49 DIVNL M.V.S. DDVS visits the section	
do	4.7.16		Routine. despatch 15 cases. To No. 7 VET HOS. Visit all units in HEDAUVILLE	
TOUTENCOURT	5.7.16		Routine visit & inspected 109 INF BDE with A.D.V.S. Transfer 10 men sent from BASE to O.C. 49 DIVNL M.V.S. dispose of unserviceable horse for 150 Frcs. Section moves to TOUTENCOURT	
do	6.7.16		Routine. A.D.V.S visits section	
do	7.7.16		Routine. sent mess cart to DHQ take over charge of 108th FLD AMB. Paid men.	
do	8.7.16		Routine. A.D.V.S. visits section	
do	9.7.16		Routine send 13 animals to No 7 VET HOS. dispose one horse met one mule unserviceable to VAASTE. DOULLENS for 300 Frcs Return STEWARTS CLIPPERS to ORDNANCE	
BEAUMETZ	10.7.16		Section moves to BEAUMETZ	
AUXI-LE-CHATEAU	11.7.16		Section moves to AUXI-LES-CHATEAU - 2-30 AM	
BLARINGHEM	12.7.16		Section moves to BLARINGHEM	
TILQUES	13.7.16		Section moves to TILQUES	
do	14.7.16		Routine. Take over Charge of 109 INF BDE No 1 & 4 Coy A.S.C. & 150 FLD Co RE Visit & inspect Same.	

WAR DIARY
or
INTELLIGENCE SUMMARY

(Erase heading not required.)

Army Form C. 2118

Place	Date	Hour	Summary of Events and Information	Remarks and references to Appendices
TILQUES	15.7.16		Routine. Drew 1000 FRCS from FIELD CASHIER	
do	16.7.16		Routine. Sent for horse at LOTTINGHEM first horse already collected - Pay men	
do	17.7.16		Routine. Outbreak of FEVER in 9 RINNIS. FUS visit & inspect 109 BDE + N° 1 Coy ASC	
do	18.7.16		Routine. Visit D. BATTY. RHA. Report on transference in diagnosis of cases to ADVS. Sent 23 cases to N°23 VET. HOS.	
do	19.7.16		Routine Visit & inspect N° 1 Coy + A Coy ASC + 109 BDE Take over Vet'y Charge of 71st BATTY RFA + inspect Same Receive 1 SUS MANGE case from N° 3 Coy ASC	
do	20.7.16		Routine. despatch 6 cases to N° 23 VETY. HOSPITAL	
LEDRINGHAM	21.7.16		Section moves to LEDRINGHAM Visit & inspect N° 121 + 122 FLD. COY. RES	
CROIX ROUGE	22.7.16		Section moves to CROIX ROUGE inspect 4 Coy ASC + 109 INF BDE	
BAILLEUL	23.7.16		Section moves to BAILLEUL area.	
	24.7.16		Section take over from 32 M.V.S. clean 6 sick animals	
	25.7.16		Routine Take over, examine, + distribute 79 Remounts. Take over Vet'y Charge. 107 INF BDE + 121 FLD Coy RE Collect horse from WESTHOF FARM
	26.7.16		Routine. Take over 2 SECT D.A.C. visit & inspect all units under vet'y charge.	
	27.7.16		Routine. Collect sick horse from FLÊTRE	
	28.7.16		Routine sent five horses to N°. 23 VET HOSPITAL	
	29.7.16		Routine Rifle + Gas Helmet inspection Try Camel. under my Vet'y Charge.	
	30.7.16		Routine. Member of COURT MARTIAL at DAC. H.Q. QRS on SGT BELL. A.V.C. See indorsed bony for 90 francs to BOUCHERIE BAILLEUL	
	31.7.16		Routine. Paid men	

WAR DIARY or INTELLIGENCE SUMMARY

Army Form C. 2118.

Vol II

OFFICER COMMANDING
No. MV4/504
Date 31.8.16
MOBILE VETERINARY SEC

Place	Date	Hour	Summary of Events and Information	Remarks and references to Appendices
B4.D.94 Sheet 36.	1.8.16		Routine and. 6 cases by canal. & 3.6 by road to No 23 VETY HOSPITAL. Visit & inspect No 2 SECT. D.A.C. admit SUS MANGE case from "C" Batty. 153 BDE. RFA	
do	2.8.16		Routine. Visit all units under Vety charge. B'isenfeld farm. Inspected with MANGE at T.30.A.0.2.	
do	3.8.16		Routine. Report on disinfection of farm for MANGE to A.D.V.S. who inspects same. collect another fro 10. for horse sale to BOUCHERIE DAILLEUL.	
do	4.8.16		Routine and. SGT JAMES + 2 MEN. + 4 cases to 23 VETY. HOS. by canal. Return 16 ADVS.	
do	5.8.16		Routine SE No 17189. PTE BOSWELL.H.H. taken on strength from No 23 VETY. HOS. No 8471. A/SERGT. SCHOLFIELD W.H. admitted to 110 FLD AMB.	
do	6.8.16		Routine. Visit all units under Vet's charge.	
do	7.8.16		Routine. admit SUS MANGE case from 173 BDE R.F.A. & 1 case from No 2 Coy. A.S.C. No 2484 PTE BRICKELL.E admitted to 110. FLD AMB.	
do	8.8.16		Routine. Panel men. 6 horses + 2 mules evacuated by BARGE to No 23. VETY. HOSPITAL. Proceed with 24 horses by road to No 23.VTY.HOS. ST OMER, T conducting party for same	

JBC

Army Form C. 2118.

WAR DIARY
or
INTELLIGENCE SUMMARY

(Erase heading not required.)

Instructions regarding War Diaries and Intelligence Summaries are contained in F.S. Regs., Part II. and the Staff Manual respectively. Title Pages will be prepared in manuscript.

OFFICER COMMANDING
No. M.V.4/804
Date 31.8.16
18T MOBILE VETERINARY SECTION

Place	Date	Hour	Summary of Events and Information	Remarks and references to Appendices
B.1.D.94 Sheet 36	9.8.16		Sick horses move from No.1 SICK HORSE HALT at VIEUX BERQUIN to 2ND. SICK HORSE HALT at EBBLINGHAM.	
	10.8.16		Hand over horses at No.23 VETY HOS. & return to No.2 SICK HORSE HALT.	
	11.8.16		Return to Section. ADVS inspect new site for M.V.S. No 11519. PTE WARNER. J. Arrived & 110. FLD. AMB. with REG. PAYMASTER in error, in the pay A/c.	
	12.8.16		Routine. SERGT. JAMES. C. animal attached from No 717. 107 M.G.C. with No. PUNCT. O.H. — DIED P.M. Shewed SEPTICAEMIA.	
	13.8.16		Routine. Sent front for arrival of 1/1 WESSEX. R.G.A. inspect all units under Vet's charge.	
	14.8.16		Routine. Return to No.1. COY. A.S.C. 1 charger cruised. and nucleus 26.7.16 with SUS MANGE Report to A.D.V.S. dearth of horse in Inf. also nature of P.M. also unit no SUS MANGE case from 150 FIELD COY R.E. report same to ADVS.	
	15.8.16		Routine. Return to NP.1. COY A.S.C. 1.HD cruised, one SUS MANGE case from 9. R. IRISH. FUS. report same to ADVS. also cases on RIDER from 1st FLD.Co.RE	

Army Form C. 2118.

WAR DIARY
or
INTELLIGENCE SUMMARY

(Erase heading not required.)

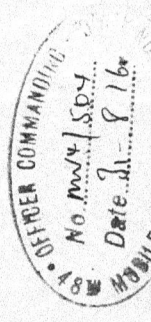

Place	Date	Hour	Summary of Events and Information	Remarks and references to Appendices
B.I.D. G.4. Sheet 36	16.8.16		Routine. Paid men. Examine horses reported scabby taken from horses of No 2 Coy A.S.C. with SUS MANGE. Result - Negative.	
do.	17.8.16		Routine. 1 NCO & 2 men to ADVS 41ST DIVN. Inspect all mules war Vety. charge.	
S.15.c.9.7. Sheet 2 a.	18.8.16		Section moves to S.15.c.9.7. Sheet 28. Chaplain 5 horse cases moved to 23 VET. HOS. Send 1 NCO i/c BOAT conducting same.	
do	19.8.16		Routine. A/SERGT SCHOLFIELD returns from 110 FLD AMB. duty-am of his mountable horses to DESCHILDRE fr. from 22S	
do	20.8.16		Routine. A.D.V.S. visit station. sent name for charge to ADVS	
do	21.8.16		Routine. Vety. Unit at unit under Vety. charge. Take over Vety. charge of all units in BAILLEUL	
do	22.8.16		Routine. and 1 case by large & 17 by Roads to 23. VET. HOS. Visit & inspect "D" ECHELON. D.A.C. with ADVS	
do	23.8.16		Routine. admit on SUS MANGE cases from 11 R. INNIS. FUS. T report same to ADVS. forwarded to ADVS AF B119. for promotion of S.S. DINSDALE Paid men. Draw 500 frs from FIELD CASHIER.	

WAR DIARY
or
INTELLIGENCE SUMMARY

(Erase heading not required.)

Army Form C. 2118.

Instructions regarding War Diaries and Intelligence Summaries are contained in F. S. Regs., Part II. and the Staff Manual respectively. Title Pages will be prepared in manuscript.

[Stamp: OFFICER COMMANDING No. MV4/SD4 Date 31-8-16 MOBILE VETERINARY SEC...]

Place	Date	Hour	Summary of Events and Information	Remarks and references to Appendices
S.15.c.9.7 Sheet 28.	24.8.16		Rendine. met 9 cases. to 23 VETY HOSPITAL by horse. Visit & inspect all units under Vety charge.	
do	25.8.16		Routine. D.D.V.S visit again. returns to A.D.V.S	
do	26.8.16		Routine. took over. examined & distributed 40 Remounts to units of 36 DIVN.	
do	27.8.16		Routine. Nos SE 16566 BOWDEN.J & SE 16583 CAUNCE.J.H transferred from 23. VETY HOS. Dépôt of unserviceable horses to DESCHILDRE. BAILLEUL. ℅ 100/A/SERGT DUNLOP transferred	
do	28.8.16		Routine. Visit all units under Vety charge. drew rations from RE for standing & half. Collect horses from VICTOR. DACQUEART. BAILLEUL by feear	
do	29.8.16		Routine. C.R.E visit section & inspect new site for sick horses standing. Evacuated 7 sick cases from "B" ECHELON. D.A.C. & to No 23. VET HOS. to unit 10 sick cases from "B" ECHELON. D.A.C. & from. BAILLEUL 3c DIV TRN. collect stray horse from. DACQUEART. SAVAGE. BAILLEUL	
do	30.8.16		Routine. Paid men disposal of one unserviceable horse in DESCHILDRE ADVS vets section.	
do	31.8.16		Routine. visit & inspect all units under Vety charge, evacuate 9 cases by horse to No 23. VETY HOS. & entraining Sant.	JK

WAR DIARY or **INTELLIGENCE SUMMARY**

Army Form C. 2118.

48th Mobile Veterinary Section — A.D.V.S. Ulster Division

Place	Date	Hour	Summary of Events and Information	Remarks and references to Appendices
Bailleul	1/9/16	A.M.	Routine, visit & inspect 108, 109, 110 Field Ambulance with A.D.V.S.	
		P.M.	Evacuate 10 cases by road to No 23 Vety Hospital. Visit & inspect Brd Sig Co RE, attend conference at A.D.V.S office.	
"	2/9/16	A.M.	Routine visit & inspect B. Echelon 36 S.T.C. with A.D.V.S.	
		P.M.	Visit & inspect 7 Labour Battalion with A.D.V.S. Some surplus animals to units.	
"	3/9/16	A.M.	Routine. Visit & inspect all Hqr. horses with A.D.V.S. admit 1 case of suspected mange from Hqr 153 Bde R.F.A.	
		P.M.	Routine.	
"	4/9/16	A.M.	Routine Visit & inspect 2nd ARMY WORKSHOPS, horses Two Carpenters taken in the strength for the purpose of building horse standings.	
		P.M.	Routine. A.D.V.S. visits section & inspects horses for evacuation.	
"	5/9/16	A.M.	Routine, evacuate 7 sick horses by barge to 23 Vety. Hospital. Visit & inspect Brd Hqr horses, R.A, Bird Sig Co RE, & 110 Field Ambulance	

A J Chase Capt RAVC

Army Form C. 2118.

WAR DIARY
or
INTELLIGENCE SUMMARY

(Erase heading not required.)

Place	Date	Hour	Summary of Events and Information	Remarks and references to Appendices
Bailleul	5/9/16	P.M.	Visit inspect 7 Labour Batt. horses, admit 1 case of suspected Mange from "B" Batty. 154 Bde.	
	6/9/16	A.M.	Routine visit inspect 109 & field Ambulance, B Echelon 36 D.A.C. 1st AUSTRALIAN TUNNELING COY.	
		P.M.	Pay men, visit inspect 2nd ARMY WORKSHOPS. Commence erection of Covered standings for sick horses. Collect stray mule belonging to 14 corps	
	7/9/16	A.M.	Routine, A.D.V.S. Van's section, send unserviceable horse to Nichilini received 125 for same. Routine.	
		P.M.	Send 9 sick animals by barge to 23 VETY. HOSPITAL. 1st Kyo horse Field Lig. Co. 105 field	
	8/9/16	A.M.	Routine Visit inspect 13 sick animals to NO 23 VETY AMBULANCE horses, dispatch 13 sick animals to NO. 23 VETY HOSPITAL.	
		P.M.	Routine. Attend conference at A.D.V.S. Office.	
	9/9/16	A.M.	Routine Visit inspect 109 FLD. AMBULANCE.	
		P.M.	Routine. inspect remount with DAF&QMG 36.4 div. Send 1 case to 12 Vety. HOSPITAL.	

A Chown Capt MC

Army Form C. 2118.

WAR DIARY
or
INTELLIGENCE SUMMARY
(Erase heading not required.)

Place	Date	Hour	Summary of Events and Information	Remarks and references to Appendices
Billeul	10/9/16	A.M.	Visit & inspect 110 Field Ambulance, 7th Labour Battalion, 2nd Army Workshops, & 1st Australian Tunnelling Coy. horses.	
		P.M.	Collect 2 chargers from Field Remount Section.	
"	11/9/16	A.M.	Routine. Draw manual for Remounts for convoy standings.	
		P.M.	ADVS visit sick horses sick horses for vaccine to 2 3 V.H.	
			Admit 1 case suspected mange from A. Batty. 153 Bde R.F.A.	
	12/9/16	A.M.	Routine. Visit & inspect. horses J unit. J 36 & Bn J.R. Div H.Q.s, Hqrs RA, Div Sig Co	
			Brand 100 horses J unit, J 36 Bn J.R.	
		P.M.	Visit & inspect Hqrs DAC. & B Echelon. 36 DAC.	
	13/9/16	A.M.	Routine. Cheque J horse to Bethune for 100 francs. ADVS visit Sailleul bath.	
			Section inspect sick horses. Washing horses for men at Sailleul bath.	
		P.M.	Paid men. Draw 500 francs from Field Cashier.	
			Routine. Visit & inspect 2nd Army Workshops, & 1st Australian	
	14/9/16	A.M.	Tunnelling Coy. with ADVS. Send 7 sick horses to 23 Vety Hospital by barge.	
			From J horse to Bethune for 125 francs.	

J. Hobson Capt M

2449 Wt. W14957/M90 750,000 1/16 J.B.C. & A. Forms/C.2118/12.

Army Form C. 2118.

WAR DIARY
or
INTELLIGENCE SUMMARY
(Erase heading not required.)

Place	Date	Hour	Summary of Events and Information	Remarks and references to Appendices
Bailleul	14/9/16	P.M.	Routine. Visit & inspect 109 Field Ambulance	
	15/9/16	A.M.	Routine. Visit & inspect 7" Lakow Bath. Visit Sg. Coy. 110 Field Ambulance & Div. HQrs. Inspect model trenching at LOCRE.	
		P.M.	Send ambulance bus to Lechilde to attend Conference at A.D.S. Office.	
	16/9/16	A.M.	Routine. Attend lecture at Divisional Anti Gas School re use of Box respirator. Visit & inspect 13 ECHELON 36 R.F.C.	
		P.M.	Routine. Visit & inspect 108 Field Ambulance. 13 ECHELON. 87 horses branded.	
	17/9/16	A.M.	Routine. Visit & inspect detail horses at 13 Echelon with A.D.V.S.	
		P.M.	Stoney. LO horse suffering from TETANUS. Hand over R. Echelon Y Hqr. bAC to Capt Shaw A.V.C.	
	18.9/16	A.M.	Routine. Baths for men at Bailleul. Hand over remainder of Units in Bailleul to Capt Shaw A.V.C.	
		P.M.	Routine	

J. Chown Capt

Army Form C. 2118.

WAR DIARY
or
INTELLIGENCE SUMMARY
(Erase heading not required.)

Instructions regarding War Diaries and Intelligence Summaries are contained in F. S. Regs., Part II. and the Staff Manual respectively. Title Pages will be prepared in manuscript.

Place	Date	Hour	Summary of Events and Information	Remarks and references to Appendices
Bailleul	19/9/16	A.M.	Routine. Evacuated 13 animals by barge to 23rd VETY. HOSPITAL.	
	20/9/16	G.M.	CAPT. CHOWN proceeded on leave. Admitted two suspected mange cases from B. ECHELON. Report same to A.D.V.S. Inspected horses of R.A. Details. CAPT. SHAW taken over duties of CAPT CHOWN while on leave.	
	21/9/16	A.M.	Routine. Evacuated 60 horses for Debility to 23rd VETY. HOSPITAL	
			Admit one suspected Mange case from 1/1 Wessex R.G.A. + report same. Evacuate 5 animals by barge to 23rd VETY. HOSPITAL.	
		P.M.	Routine. Visit + inspect 108 FIELD AMBULANCE	
	22/9/16	A.M.	Routine. Send horse from D.D.V.S. 2nd Army to Deschilde for destruction.	
		P.M.	Attend conference at A.D.V.S. Office + render weekly such returns.	
	23/9/16	A.M.	Routine. One incurable horse sent to Deschilde for destruction.	
		P.M.	Routine. Visit + Inspect Div. Sig. Coy. + Div. Hqrs.	

J. Chown Capt. MC

Army Form C. 2118.

WAR DIARY
or
INTELLIGENCE SUMMARY

(Erase heading not required.)

Place	Date	Hour	Summary of Events and Information	Remarks and references to Appendices
	24/9/16	A.M.	Routine. Visit & inspect 109th FIELD AMBULANCE.	
		P.M.	Routine.	
	25/9/16	A.M.	Routine. Visit 108th FIELD AMBULANCE.	
		P.M.	Routine.	
	26/9/16	A.M.	Routine. Evacuate 6 animals by barge to 23rd Vety. Hospital. Also 46 animals by road to 23rd Vety. Hospital	
		P.M.	Routine. D.D.V.S. 2nd Army visited & inspected this Section.	
	27/9/16	A.M.	Routine. Visit Vinyard Kil Hqrs Y Hqrs R.A.	
		P.M.	Routine.	
	28/9/16	A.M.	Routine. evacuate 17 animals by barge to 23 Vety Hospital.	
		P.M.	Send unserviceable horse to Sechelaire Bailleul Capt Chown return from leave.	
	29/9/16	A.M.	Routine. Visit & inspect 61st Hqrs Y Hqrs R.A.	
		P.M.	Return to A.D.V.S.	
	30/9/16	A.M.	Routine. Visit Inspect. 109 Field Ambulance. 108 Field Ambulance.	
		P.M.	Paid.	

H Chinn Capt AVC.
Comdg. 48th Mobile Vety Section

Army Form C. 2118.

WAR DIARY
or
INTELLIGENCE SUMMARY

48th Mobile Vety Section

Vol R

(Erase heading not required.)

Place	Date	Hour	Summary of Events and Information	Remarks and references to Appendices
BAILLEUL.	1.10.16	A.M.	Routine. Drew 500 francs from Field Cashier. Hand over all work under Vety Charge of Capt Shaw to Capt. WHYTE.	
		P.M.	Routine. Visit CRE re material for standings	
	2.10.16	A.M.	Routine. A.D.V.S. visits section. Visit & inspect Div Hqrs, Hqrs RA, Y Div Sig Coy. Drew 250 francs from BECHLORÉ for lito unwounded animals	
		P.M.	Routine. Bathing parade for men	
	3.10.16	A.M.	Routine. Send eight sick animals by barge to 23 VETY. HOSPITAL.	
		P.M.	Routine. Visit & inspect 109 FIELD AMBULANCE.	
	4.10.16	A.M.	Proceed 1/o9 Special Train to NEUFCHATEL to No 13 VETY. HOSPITAL with 200 sick animals of 7th, 36th, & 16th Divisions	
	5.10.16	A.M.	Return with conducting party to Unit.	
	6.10.16	AM	Routine. A.D.V.S. visit Section. Visit & inspect 108 FIELD AMBULANCE	
		PM	Routine. Return to A.D.V.S. attend conference & give a lecture in use of new box respirator	
	7.10.16	A.M.	Routine. Visit & inspect. Kw1t Hqr, Hqrs RA Y & to Ly 6 R.E.	
		P.M.	Routine. Y Ambulance. 21 Remounts at Rathred	

Army Form C. 2118.

WAR DIARY
or
INTELLIGENCE SUMMARY

(Erase heading not required.)

Instructions regarding War Diaries and Intelligence Summaries are contained in F. S. Regs., Part II. and the Staff Manual respectively. Title Pages will be prepared in manuscript.

Place	Date	Hour	Summary of Events and Information	Remarks and references to Appendices
BAILLEUL.	8.10.16	A.M.	Routine. Evacuate. 10 sick animals to 23 Vety. Hospital.	
		P.M.	Routine. Exch. new kit for men.	
"	9.10.16	A.M.	Routine. Visit & inspect kit C.G.Cy. R.E.	
		P.M.	Routine. Sent subscription to Kitchener Memorial Fund to A.D.V.S.	
	10.10.16	A.M.	Routine. Send 12 sick animals to 23 Vety. Hospital. Visit & inspect	
			109 Field Ambulance.	
		P.M.	Routine. Visit & check charges from Field Remount Section. with A.D.V.S.	
	11.10.16	A.M.	Routine. Visit & inspect 108 Fld Fd Ambulance. Visit inspect Mgr R.A. 75th Bgr.	
		P.M.	Routine. Bathing parade for men. Evac 125 frames from Bechelare. Balla	
	12.10.16	A.M.	Routine. arrange for new walk supply to section.	
		P.M.	Routine. Communion holding. 2 frames am stamping shed.	
	13.10.16	A.M.	Routine. Send 10 sick horse to 23 Vety. Hospital by barge.	
		P.M.	Routine. Visit inspect 109 Field Ambulance	
	14.10.16	A.M.	Routine. Paid men. Evac 500 frames from Field Cphn.	
		P.M.	Routine. Send frames from stamping shed.	

WAR DIARY
or
INTELLIGENCE SUMMARY

Army Form C. 2118.

Place	Date	Hour	Summary of Events and Information	Remarks and references to Appendices
BAILLEUL	15.10.16	A.M.	Routine. Depart 19 Pin Annual to 23 Vety. Hospital	
		P.M.	Routine. Visit inspected kut Hqr, Hqr RA & Bd. Sig Coy	
	16.10.16	A.M.	Routine. Visit inspected 108 Field Ambulance	
		P.M.	Routine. Visit 108 Bde M.G. Coy.	
	17.10.16	A.M.	Routine. Departed 6 by annual to No 23 Vety. Hospital	
		P.M.	Routine. Bathing parade for men.	
	19.10.16	A.M.	Routine. Visit inspected kit Hqrs, Hqrs RA Bde Sig & C RE	
		P.M.	Routine. ADVS visits & chn to give opening lecture to AVC Sergeants.	
	19.10.16	A.M.	Routine. Evacuate 5 sick animals to 23 Vety. Hospital	
		P.M.	Routine. Visit & inspect 108 Field Ambulance & attend a conference at ADVS office	
	20.10.16	A.M.	Routine. Visit inspect. 2nd Hqr RA. visit by C RE	
		P.M.	Routine. Attend a conference ADVS office.	
	21.10.16	A.M.	Routine. Medical inspection for men.	
		P.M.	Routine. Visit inspect 169 Field Ambulance	

WAR DIARY
or
INTELLIGENCE SUMMARY

Army Form C. 2118.

Place	Date	Hour	Summary of Events and Information	Remarks and references to Appendices
Bailleul 22-11	22.10.16	A.M.	Routine. Collect sick horses by float from MERRIS.	
		P.M.	Routine. Take over horses from Field Remount Section	
	23.10.16	A.M.	Routine. Take over duties of Adv. 36 Kn. & Major Horner on leave. Bath for men.	
		P.M.	Routine. Take over & Auditated 46 Remounts to work of 16 K Batt.	
	24.10.16	A.M.	Routine. Send 9 sick animals to 23 Vety. Hospital.	
		P.M.	Routine. Visit & inspect 108 Field Ambulance	
	25.10.16	A.M.	Routine. Visit & inspect 109 Field Ambulance, Div. Hqrs, Hq RA VDiv. Sig. Co.	
		P.M.	Routine. Lecture to AVC Sergeants & drivers on stable management.	
	26.10.16	A.M.	Routine. Pte Hartt admitted to hospital.	
		P.M.	Routine.	
	27.10.16	A.M.	Routine. Despatch 5 sick animals to 23 Vety. Hospital	
		P.M.	Routine. Idea Conference in place of A.D.V.S.	
	28.00.10	A.M.	Routine. Visit & inspect 109 Field Ambulance	
		P.M.	Routine. Pay men draw fresh from JGCD Cashier, before J unavailable horse K Sechepet for 150 francs.	

Army Form C. 2118.

WAR DIARY
or
INTELLIGENCE SUMMARY
(Erase heading not required.)

Place	Date	Hour	Summary of Events and Information	Remarks and references to Appendices
BAILLEUL	29/10/16	A.M.	Routine. Visit & inspect. B8 Hqrs. Hqr RE, RA, 1 Div. Sig. Coy.	
		P.M.	Routine.	
	30/10/16	A.M.	Routine. Visit & inspect 108 Field Ambulance	
		P.M.	Routine. Baths for men	
	31/10/16	A.M.	Routine evacuated 16 sick animals to 23 Vety. Hospital	
		P.M.	Routine. Visit & inspect 109 Field Ambulance	

J.Chester
Capt AVC
Commanding
48 MVS.

WAR DIARY
INTELLIGENCE SUMMARY

Army Form C. 2118.

A.D.V.S
Mod Vety Sec
@ irgway
Vol 14

Place	Date	Hour	Summary of Events and Information	Remarks and references to Appendices
BAILLEUL	1.11.16	A.M.	Routine. Visit & inspect 109 Field Ambulance. Take over Vety Charge of 2nd Anzac Corps Hqrs.	
		P.M.	Routine. Declined to AVC reports	
	2.11.16	A.M.	Routine. ADVS. taken over Vety Charge of division on return from leave	
		P.M.	Routine. Visit & inspect 108 Field Ambulance	
	3.8.16	A.M.	Routine. Visit & inspect Bde Hqrs, Agn RA, RE, Y Div Sig Coy, Y Div 2 M Anzac Corp Hqrs	
		P.M.	Routine. Attend Conference at ADVS office. Visit & inspect Div F150	
	4.11.16	A.M.	Routine. Dispose of unserviceable horse to stables	
		P.M.	Routine. Visit & inspect 109 Field Ambulance	
	5.11.16	A.M.	Routine. Visit & inspect 108 Field Ambulance. Sec Hqrs Agn RA, 2nd Bn Lr Co. V Agn RE	
		P.M.	Routine. Paid men	
	6.11.16	A.M.	Routine. Baths for men	J.C. (in)
		P.M.	Routine. ADVS had & inspect sections	J.C.

WAR DIARY or INTELLIGENCE SUMMARY

Army Form C. 2118.

Place	Date	Hour	Summary of Events and Information	Remarks and references to Appendices
BAILLEUL	7.11.16	A.M.	Routine. Inspect Q. inconvenable to BECKLERE for J. 150	
		P.M.	Routine	
	8.11.16	A.M.	Routine. Inspect stablette 23 Reserves 6 hrs J. Duncan	
		P.M.	Routine. Lecture to A.V.C. Sergeants on Stable management	
	9.11.16	A.M.	Routine. Visit & inspect 109 Field AMBULANCE	
		P.M.	Routine. Visit & inspect 108 FIELD AMBULANCE	
	10.11.16	A.M.	Routine. Inspect Q. inconvenable horse to DESCHILDRE BAILLEUL for J.150	
	11.11.16	A.M.	Routine. attend conference at A.D.V.S. office. Visit & inspect Div. Hqrs, Hq. R.A, R.E, Y & W. Sig. Coy.	
		P.M.	Routine. Bathing parade for men	
	12.11.16	A.M.	Routine. Medical inspection for men	
		P.M.	Routine. Clothing horse belong. to French civilian	
	13.11.16	A.M.	Routine. Visit & inspect 109 Field Ambulance. Bathing parade for men	
		P.M.	Routine. Give a lecture on Stable management to officers & drivers	

Army Form C. 2118.

WAR DIARY
or
INTELLIGENCE SUMMARY

(Erase heading not required.)

Instructions regarding War Diaries and Intelligence Summaries are contained in F. S. Regs., Part II. and the Staff Manual respectively. Title Pages will be prepared in manuscript.

Place	Date	Hour	Summary of Events and Information	Remarks and references to Appendices
BAILLEUL	14.11.16	A.M.	Routine. Evacuate 8 horses by trps & 22 by road to No 23 VETY. HOSPITAL	
		P.M.	Routine. No 13972 Pte Clarke W. taken in strength from No 13 VETY. HOSPITAL deliver a lecture on Stable management to officers & Anvers.	
	15.11.16	A.M.	Routine. Visit & inspect 108 Field Ambulance	
		P.M.	Routine. Lecture to N.V.C. Sergeants. Lecture to Officers & Anvers of Stable management.	
	16.11.16	A.M.	Routine. A.D.V.S visit & inspected Sick. Commence history of nostalia &c for Contagion disease	
		P.M.	Routine. Lecture to officers on Stable management	
	17.11.16	A.M.	Routine. Visit & inspect Adv. Hqs. Hqrs. R.A., R.E. & Div by C.C. R.E.	
		P.M.	Routine. Attend conference at A.D.V.S. Office. Lecture on Stable management.	
	18/11/16	A.M.	Routine. Visit & inspect 108 Field Ambulance. Paid men.	
		P.M.	Routine. Lecture on Stable management. Drew 500 frans for fees Captain	J Nelson

Army Form C. 2118.

WAR DIARY
or
INTELLIGENCE SUMMARY

(Erase heading not required.)

Instructions regarding War Diaries and Intelligence Summaries are contained in F. S. Regs., Part II. and the Staff Manual respectively. Title Pages will be prepared in manuscript.

Place	Date	Hour	Summary of Events and Information	Remarks and references to Appendices
BAILEUL	19/11/16	A.M.	Routine. Medical inspection for men	
		P.M.	Routine	
	20.11.16	A.M.	Routine. Visit & inspect 108 FIELD AMBULANCE. Bath for men	
		P.M.	Routine. Gave a practical demonstration in stable management to officers of trench Mortar Commander inspects. Two horse shot with protective plate for sole and Hgs, Hgs RE, Hgs RA & Div Sig Co RE.	
	21.11.16	A.M.	Routine. Visit & inspect Arti Hgs, Hgs, RE, Hgs, RA & DIV Sig Co RE.	
		P.M.	Routine. Clothing inspection for men	
	22.11.16	A.M.	Routine. Visit & inspect 109 FIELD AMBULANCE	
		P.M.	Routine. Lecture to A.V.C. Sergeant on Rabble "management"	
	23.11.16	A.M.	Routine. Sarcopti parasite found in scrapings taken from no 2 section B.A.C. Same reported to A.D.V.S. V.O. i/c	
		P.M.	Routine. Admit 4 propelled mange cases from B.BATTY. 173 Bde. RFA	
	24.11.16	A.M.	Routine. Evacuated 8 sick animals to 23 VETY. HOSPITAL	
		P.M.	Routine. Attend conference A.D.V.S. office.	
	25.11.16	A.M.	Routine. Draw 1000 francs from FIELD CASHIER	
		P.M.	Routine. Pay men DDVS & ADVS inspect section	

Army Form C. 2118.

WAR DIARY
or
INTELLIGENCE SUMMARY

(Erase heading not required.)

Instructions regarding War Diaries and Intelligence Summaries are contained in F. S. Regs., Part II. and the Staff Manual respectively. Title Pages will be prepared in manuscript.

Place	Date	Hour	Summary of Events and Information	Remarks and references to Appendices
BAILLEUL	26/11/16	AM	Routine. Medical inspection of men. Visit Transport 109 FIELD AMBULANCE	
		P.M.	Routine. ADMS, visit section.	
	27/11/16	AM	Routine. Baths for men. Visit Transport 108 FIELD AMBULANCE	
		P.M.	Routine	
	28/11/16	AM	Routine. Saw over 39 Remount & examine & establish same send 15 men to 22 VETY. HOSPITAL by road. Send 12 by CANAL to 23 V.H.	
		P.M.	Routine	
	29/11/16	A.M.	Routine. Visit Transport 109 FIELD AMBULANCE	
		P.M.	Routine. Examination for AVC Sergeants	
	30/11/16	AM	Routine. Visit & inspect Bn Hqrs, Hq RA, RE & van S.S. Co	
		P.M.	Routine	

WAR DIARY or INTELLIGENCE SUMMARY

Army Form C. 2118.

Vol 15

Place	Date	Hour	Summary of Events and Information	Remarks and references to Appendices
BAILLEUL	1/12/16	AM	Routine Capt DAVIDSON proceed on leave, draws £500 from FIELD. CASHIER	
		PM	Routine attend conference ADVS Ypres	
	2/12/16	A.M.	Routine Visit surgical Kal Hqs. Hqs RA, RE Hal Sig. Co	
		P.M.	Routine Paid men	
	3/12/16	A.M.	Routine. Visit surgical 109 FIELD AMBULANCE	
		P.M.	Routine Take over Veterinary Charge of Hqs 2nd ANZAC Corps. Medical inspection for men	
	4/12/16	AM	Routine. Visit surgical 2nd ANZAC CORPS HQRS, 108 FIELD AMBULANCE	
		PM	Routine ADVS visit return. Visit 2ND ANZAC CORPS, HQRS	
	5/12/16	AM	Routine depart 10 animals to 23 Vety HOSPITAL	
		PM	Routine admit care of suspected mange from C Batt. 173 Bde.	
	6/12/16	A.M.	Routine Visit surgical 108 FIELD AMBULANCE	
		P.M.	Routine ADVS visit return. Inspect AVC sergeants	
	7/12/16	A.M.	Routine	

Army Form C. 2118.

WAR DIARY
or
INTELLIGENCE SUMMARY
(Erase heading not required.)

Instructions regarding War Diaries and Intelligence Summaries are contained in F. S. Regs., Part II. and the Staff Manual respectively. Title Pages will be prepared in manuscript.

Place	Date	Hour	Summary of Events and Information	Remarks and references to Appendices
Baileul	8/12/16	AM	Routine. Visit & inspect two HQrs. HQRS RA, RE & 2nd Fd Coy. Send party two remounts at Railhead. depart Journal to 2.3 Vety. HOSPITAL.	
		PM	Routine. PMO here. Malc died nearest Clover Laurence. Parade at approach of H.Q.? despace of unserviceable horse to Sechilini for F.SO	
	9/12/16	AM	Routine. Inspires of 1 unserviceable horse & 1 unserviceable mule to Sechilini for F.260. horse F.560 from Wild Cashier	
		P.M.	Routine. paid men attend approach for A.D.V.S. at two "Train Hqrs." proceed to FIELD REMOUNT SECTION & took over Remount	
	10/12/16	AM	Routine. Medical inspection for men Vieil Rempart 2nd Dragon Corps Hqrs	
		PM	Routine. Visit rempart 109 Field Ambulance	
	11/12/16	AM	Routine	
		P.M.	Routine	
	12/12/16	AM	Routine. dispatch 15 Cht. Animal to 23 Vety. HOSPITAL.	
		PM	Routine. Taken over charge of A.D.V.S. during his illness	

J Chester
(O i/c ARVC)

Army Form C. 2118.

WAR DIARY
or
INTELLIGENCE SUMMARY

(Erase heading not required.)

Instructions regarding War Diaries and Intelligence Summaries are contained in F.S. Regs., Part II and the Staff Manual respectively. Title Pages will be prepared in manuscript.

Place	Date	Hour	Summary of Events and Information	Remarks and references to Appendices
BAILLEUL	13/12/16	A.M.	Routine admin me inspected horses from 153 Bde R.F.A.	
		P.M.	Routine visit & inspect of Hqrs 2ND ANZAC CORPS. ADMS inspected section	
	14/12/16	AM	Routine Baths for men visit & inspect 109 Field Ambulance	
		PM	Routine Disposal of 1 unserviceable mare to Bechford Bailleul from F.150	
	15/12/16	AM	Routine - Reported 10 horses to 23 Vety Hospital by rays	
		PM	Routine - Presided at enquiries ADVS Nice	
	16/12/16	AM	Routine Visit transport 2nd Hqrs Hqrs RA RE Ptbl Sy G	
		PM	Routine Paid men	
	17/12/16	AM	Routine Visit inspect 108 FIELD AMBULANCE	
		PM	Routine. Visit inspect 109 FIELD AMBULANCE	
	18/12/16	AM	Routine medical inspection 9 men	
		P.M.	Routine Baths for men	
	19/12/16	AM	Routine Vacd. inspect 2nd Hqrs Hqrs RA RE Vetd Sig. Coy.	
		P.M.	Routine inspect 9 animals to 23 Vety. Hospital.	

A.J.Brown Colonel

Army Form C. 2118.

WAR DIARY
or
INTELLIGENCE SUMMARY

(Erase heading not required.)

Instructions regarding War Diaries and Intelligence Summaries are contained in F. S. Regs., Part II and the Staff Manual respectively. Title Pages will be prepared in manuscript.

Place	Date	Hour	Summary of Events and Information	Remarks and references to Appendices
BAILLEUL	20/12/16	AM.	Routine. Visit transport 109 FIELD AMBULANCE	
		P.M.	Routine. SARCOPTIC MANGE found in 14 RIR Jane reported to ADVS.	
	21/12/16	AM	Routine. Visit & inspect 108 FIELD AMBULANCE	
		P.M.	Routine. Took over Vety Charge of IX CORPS Hosp. & M/HV 24 C CORPS from Capt FLANAGAN on leave	
	22/12/16	AM	Routine. Visit & inspect Corps Bakery	
		PM	Routine. Admit 3 cases suspected mange 170 Mchy BATT. Found at carpenters ADVS office.	
	23/12/16	AM	Routine. Evacuate 8 animals to 22 VETY HOSPITAL.	
		PM	Routine. Visit & inspect 2" AM3CC CORPS. 109 FIELD AMBULANCE Dispose of incurable horse to RECHIERE for £125. PAID keen.	
	24/12/16	AM.	Routine. Visit transport 108 FIELD AMBULANCE	
		PM	Routine. late am 24 Remount at Railhead	
	25/12/16	AM.	Routine. } same	
		PM.	Routine. }	
	26/12/16	AM	Routine. Take over horses from FIELD REMOUNT SECTION.	
		PM	Routine.	

JFCrow Capt AVC

Army Form C. 2118.

WAR DIARY
or
INTELLIGENCE SUMMARY

(Erase heading not required.)

Instructions regarding War Diaries and Intelligence Summaries are contained in F.S. Regs, Part II. and the Staff Manual respectively. Title Pages will be prepared in manuscript.

Place	Date	Hour	Summary of Events and Information	Remarks and references to Appendices
BAILLEUL	27/12/16	A.M.	Routine. Visit transport 109 Field Ambulance, Div Hqr, Sig. Co, RE	
		P.M.	IX Corps Cavalry, Hqr RE & RA. Routine. Arrang for Mobile Section.	
	28/12/16	A.M.	Routine. Visit transport Hqr. S.A.C. R Eshers 2nd Army, WSTRDSPS, 110 Field Ambulance & 1st Canadian Reserve Park.	
		P.M.	Visit transport 108 Field Ambulance	
	29/12/16	A.M.	Routine. Evacuate 27 Animals to 23 Vety Hospital, by road. also 6 by Canal to 23 V.H.	
		P.M.	Routine. Section inspected by Sanitary Officer. attend Conference AD.V.S.	
	30/12/16	A.M.	Routine. Visit transport 1 Canadian Reserve Park.	
		P.M.	Routine.	
	31/12/16	A.M.	Routine. Visit transport 2nd ANZAC Corps. H.Q.R.	
		P.M.	Routine. medical inspection for men.	

Comdg 48th Mobile Veterinary Section

WAR DIARY
or
INTELLIGENCE SUMMARY

Army Form C. 2118.

(Erase heading not required.)

Place	Date	Hour	Summary of Events and Information	Remarks and references to Appendices
BAILLEUL	1/1/17	A.M.	Routine. Visit & inspect first Ly Coy RE, HQrs RA & RE, Bn Hqrs, IX CORPS CAVALRY	
		P.M.	Routine. Cpl Parker proceeds on leave.	
	2/1/17	A.M.	Routine. Dispatch Sgt Davidson to 5 Vety Hospital. Visit & inspect. 109 Field Ambulance, HQrs SMC, B Echelon. 3rd Canadian Tunneling Coy 2nd Army Workshops	
		P.M.	Routine. Visit & inspect. 108 Field Ambulance. Paid men.	
	3/1/17	A.M.	Routine. Visit & inspect. Res Hqrs & Horselines	
		P.M.	Routine. Sarcoptic parasite found & reported ADVS. Pte Pickles taken on Strey Return.	
	4/1/16	A.M.	Routine. Visit & inspect 7 K Labour Battalion. No 9 Vety Hospital.	
		P.M.	Routine. A.D.V.S. Visit & inspects section.	
	5/1/16	A.M.	Routine. Visit & inspect 109 Field Ambulance. Dispatch 26 horses v1 roads by road to 23 Vety Hospital.	
		P.M.	Routine. dispatch 10 horses by canal to 23 Vety Hospital. Attend Conference at ADVS office.	

WAR DIARY or INTELLIGENCE SUMMARY

Army Form C. 2118.

Place	Date	Hour	Summary of Events and Information	Remarks and references to Appendices
BAILLEUL	6/1/17	A.M.	Routine. Visit & inspect 110 FIELD AMBULANCE	
		P.M.	Routine. Visit & inspect 108 FIELD AMBULANCE	
	7/1/17	A.M.	Routine. Visit. Sril. Sig. Co., Hqrs. R.E. & R.A. 2nd I/Hqrs.	
		P.M.	Routine. Visit & inspect Hqrs. BHQ, B ECHELON, 1st CANADIAN TUNNELLING Co Y.	
	8/1/16	A.M.	Deposit of 1 unrideable horse to Echelon's Strf 150. Routine. Visit & inspect bn Lg. G. Co. drew £500 from Field Cashier.	
		P.M.	Routine. Visit & inspect 108 & 109 FIELD AMBULANCES. Paid men	
	9/1/17	A.M.	Routine. Visit & inspect 2nd ARMY. WORKSHOPS, 7th LABOUR BATTALION.	
		P.M.	Routine. 2 Horses to 23 VETY. HOSPITAL, by large S returned officer. 12 bn held 1st Capt. 100 pat for Pm from 2nd ARMY WORKSHOPS.	
	10/1/17	A.M.	Visit 109 FIELD AMBULANCE Routine	
		P.M.	Routine. Attend Conference ADVS Office.	
	11/1/17	A.M.	Routine. Visit & inspect 108 FIELD AMBULANCE.	
		P.M.	Routine. attend lecture given by ADVS.	
	12/1/17	A.M.	Routine. Visit & inspect Hn. S.G.Co., D/W I/Hqr. Hqr. R.A. R.E. D/W I/Hqr. Hqr. R.A. R.E. K.23 VETY H.	
		P.M.	Routine attend Conference ADVS three Shows by Major, attend ADVS Lecture	

Army Form C. 2118.

WAR DIARY
or
INTELLIGENCE SUMMARY

(Erase heading not required.)

Place	Date	Hour	Summary of Events and Information	Remarks and references to Appendices
BAILLEUL	13/1/17	A.M.	Routine. Examine 8 Sherpen's from 13DH. 13a held a reyable result	
		P.M.	Routine. Send 1 horse to 23 Vety. Hospital by mon Ambulance	
	14/1/17	A.M.	Routine. Admit Glan. surg. mange from 130 Heavy Battery	
		P.M.	Routine. obtain 50 pack-pads & from e) ARMY. WORKSHOPS.	
	15/1/17	A.M.	Routine. Paid respect visits. Hqrs, Hqr RA, RE etc. Vis. Cy. BE	
		P.M.	Routine. Visit 2" ANZAC. CORPS. Hqt. visit our Vety. Charge. Pous nay attend demonstration by M.S.V.S. 2 horses to Steenkirk Baillie	
	16/1/17	A.M.	Routine. dispatch 28 mange cases to 23 Vety. Hospital	
		PM	Routine. Visit transpoil 108 & 109 FIELD AMBULANCES	
	17/1/17	A.M.	Routine. When B. horse to 169 MPC	
		PM	Return. Attend conference at MDVS 3pm. visit horse dep at St. Jans Cappel.	
	18/1/17	A.M.	Routine. Visit 2" ANZAC HQRS. receive £246 for hie annual refu	
		PM	Return Bailleul	

Army Form C. 2118.

WAR DIARY
or
INTELLIGENCE SUMMARY
(Erase heading not required.)

Place	Date	Hour	Summary of Events and Information	Remarks and references to Appendices
BAILLEUL	19/1/17	A.M.	Routine. ADVS insp. adm. Visit inspect. Stably 6 RE Bde HQrs. 109 RHA Bde	
		P.M.	Routine. Depart 12 Case S.E. 23 Vety. Hospital, attend conference R.S.V.S.	
	20/1/17	A.M.	Routine. Visit 2nd ANZAC Corps HQrs. changed action attacking for mange	
		P.M.	Routine	
	21/1/17	A.M.	Routine. Visit inspect. 109 Field Ambulance	
		P.M.	Routine. adsit about 50 Cases of mange	
	22/1/17	A.M.	Routine. Visit inspect with ADVS, Stably 6 RE Hqrs RE. RA. Wsh Hqrs. changed lines 7th Battery, 173 Bde R.F.A.	
		P.M.	Routine. ADVS inspect mange cases to go to base	
	23/1/17	A.M.	Routine. Dispatch 46 cases mange to 23 Vety. Hospital by road & by canal	
		P.M.	Routine. Visit men	
	24/1/17	A.M.	Routine. Visit inspect. Rest Hqrs. Kis Ly 6 RE bys RH TRE	
		P.M.	[signature] hertz P.M. 109 Field Ambulance	

WAR DIARY
or
INTELLIGENCE SUMMARY

(Erase heading not required.)

Army Form C. 2118.

Place	Date	Hour	Summary of Events and Information	Remarks and references to Appendices
Bailleul	25/1/17	A.M.	Routine. Visit transport 109 Field Ambulance 2nd ANZAC CORPS HQrs	
		P.M.	Routine. Attend conference HQrs. office	
	26/1/17	10 A.M.	Routine. Visit transport 108 Field Ambulance. Mule P.M. M.V.S. horse invalid. TRAUMATIC PERIOPHLITIS
		P.M.	Routine. Attend conference at DDVS office	
	27/1/17	A.M.	Routine. Private Sedon horn clipper at 1st Corps Corp. Visit sick unit at HQ Corps ∴ HQ Corps ∴ 1st Corps Sig. CC	
		P.M.	Routine	
	28/1/17	A.M.	Routine. Visit transport 2nd ANZAC HQrs. draw 250 f. from Kechelbe	
			for his honoraria horse	
		P.M.	Routine	
	29/1/17	A.M.	Routine. Visit transport kid Lg E. Pte. HQrs. RA.RE. & 1 HQ CC. Paid men	
		P.M.	Routine. Visit transport 108 & 109 Field Ambulances. All units. August with CG2	
	30/1/17	A.M.	Routine. Visit transport 2nd ANZAC. HQrs	
		P.M.	Routine. attend DDVS office	
	31/1/17	A.M.	Routine. Sunday. Xmas imported section	
		P.M.	Routine Lave over clicks of DSVS & Montferrin or Bruce	

48th Mobile Veterinary Section

WAR DIARY or INTELLIGENCE SUMMARY

Army Form C. 2118

Vol 17

Place	Date	Hour	Summary of Events and Information	Remarks and references to Appendices
BAILLEUL	1/2/17	A.M.	Routine. Div HQrs, Div Sig Coy HQrs RA & RE paid through IX Corps Horse Dip.	
		P.M.	Routine. Pte CLAPHAM proceed on 10 days leave. Drew 100 forms from Field Cashier	
	2/2/17	A.M.	Routine. Section inspected by AA. Q.M.G. 36 Div & Colonel of Italian Army	
		P.M.	Routine. Pte BARRAT proceed on 10 days leave	
	3/2/17	A.M.	Routine. Sergt. JAMES proceed on 10 days leave.	
		P.M.	Routine. Preside at conference ADVS office	
	4/2/17	A.M.	Routine. Pte Jago proceed on 10 days leave. Visit & inspect 2nd ANZAC CORPS HQrs	
		P.M.	Routine. dispose of unserviceable horse to Knockers Bailleul for JRS.	
	5/2/17	A.M.	Routine. Visit & inspect Bn HQrs. Bn Sy Co RE HQrs RA & RE	
		P.M.	Routine. Visit & inspect 108 Field Ambulance, 109 Field Ambulance. Paid men	
	6/2/17	A.M.	Routine. attend IX CORPS Conf	
		P.M.	Routine.	
	7/2/17	A.M.	Routine. LECTURE to AVC Sergeant on MANGE	
		P.M.	Bn HQrs Visit & inspect. Bn HQrs. Bn Sy Co RE. HQ RA RE	
	8/2/17	A.M.	Routine. Visit IX Corps Dip. dispose unserviceable horse to Knockers Bailleul for 150	

Army Form C. 2118

WAR DIARY
or
INTELLIGENCE SUMMARY
(Erase heading not required.)

Instructions regarding War Diaries and Intelligence Summaries are contained in F.S. Regs., Part II. and the Staff Manual respectively. Title Pages will be prepared in manuscript.

Place	Date	Hour	Summary of Events and Information	Remarks and references to Appendices
BAILLEUL	9/2/17	A.M.	Routine. Took on attacked Remounts for 26 Bde.	
		P.M.	Routine. Precis of experience ADVS office	
	10/2/17	A.M.	Routine. Visit transport units under Vety Charge	
		P.M.	Routine.	
	11/2/17	A.M.	Routine. Visit 2nd Anzac Corps HQrs. 2 Class Change.	
		P.M.	Routine.	
	12/2/17	A.M.	Routine. Visit transport Bn HQrs, ASC, S.R. Corps, HQrs RA, RE,	
		P.M.	Routine. Cases of wounded horse & Beckhem /25 Paid men.	
	13/2/17	A.M.	Routine. DDVS visit, action v. injured Champetier Shed.	
		P.M.	Routine. Ph Clapham returns from leave.	
	14/2/17	A.M.	Routine. Visit transport units	
		P.M.	Routine. Pass sicken annual horse Champetier Shed.	
	15/2/17	A.M.	Routine. Attend demonstration on mange at 23 Vety Hospital.	
		P.M.	Routine. Despatch 17 annual to 23 Vety Hospital.	
	16/2/17	A.M.	Routine. Visit Vety Corps, Evty. injured trsf by Co. HQrs RA & RE.	
		P.M.	Routine. Practical: Anymore ADVS office.	

Army Form C. 2118

WAR DIARY
or
INTELLIGENCE SUMMARY
(Erase heading not required.)

Instructions regarding War Diaries and Intelligence Summaries are contained in F.S. Regs., Part II. and the Staff Manual respectively. Title Pages will be prepared in manuscript.

Place	Date	Hour	Summary of Events and Information	Remarks and references to Appendices
BAILLEUL	17/2/17	AM	Routine Inspec 2nd Anz. Aux Hqrs	
		PM	Routine Sergt Garn. return from leave. Medical inspection for men	
	18/2/17	AM	Routine Visit inspected 109 FIELD Ambulance	
		PM	Routine Church Parade for men.	
	19/2/17	A.M.	Routine Visit inspected Bn.H.Qrs. HQRS RE, RA, Y5th & 6th Coy R.E.	
		P.M.	Routine Visit inspected 108 Y 109 FIELD AMBULANCES, evacuable cases to BAILHILD R.E. Fw/s0	
	20/2/17	A.M.	Routine despatch 13 sick animals by road Y 11 animals by train to 23 Vety HOSPITAL	
		P.M.	Routine disposed of evacuable cases to Bailleul for two sanitary sections to A & B 172 RFA more reinforcement My General Cavan.	
	21/2/17	A.M.	Routine Sanitary section to 130 Heavy Batt.y & 71 Heavy Batt.y RGA	
		PM	Routine	
	22/2/17	AM	Routine Visit inspected Bn.H.Qrs. HQRS RA, RE, & Bn.H.Qrs. G.R.E. Pass all Capt. Millar's Many C cases	
			hump champetre Stud (150 cases)	
			Routine Sanitar section to 9th Corps Cavalry, 1MO Y 3 men known on through J Behin	
			for Bn.H.Qrs for champetre Std.	
	23/2/17	AM	Routine Pass 150 mange cases through Brougham Stud lines, 1 case rendering hoof cast.	
		PM	Passed to 23 V.H.s WO. Evacuum of evacuable horses to Bailleul Jan 7 150 Y 125.	

1875 Wt.w W593/825 1,000,000 4/15 J.B.C. & A. A.D.S.S./Forms/C. 2118.

Army Form C. 2118

WAR DIARY
or
INTELLIGENCE SUMMARY
(Erase heading not required.)

Instructions regarding War Diaries and Intelligence Summaries are contained in F. S. Regs., Part II. and the Staff Manual respectively. Title Pages will be prepared in manuscript.

Place	Date	Hour	Summary of Events and Information	Remarks and references to Appendices
BAILLEUL	24/3/17	AM	Routine pass 112 Avres through Champcleg shed. Take on Gamma Substitute 62 Kennels	
		P.M.	Routine. F.D.V.S. work sector.	
	25/3/17	A.M.	Routine pass 90 cars through Champcleg shed. Visit Hospital 2nd Army an Corps HQrs	
		P.M.	Routine.	
	26/3/17	A.M.	Routine relinquish duties of OTSVS 36 Btn en relive of Major Jones DSO	
		P.M.	Routine pass 150 cars through Champcleg shed. Visit and inch ADVS	
	27/3/17	AM	Routine ADVS work section. despatch 24 cases to 23 VETY HOSPITAL despatch unserviceable food to S.V.H.	
		P.M.	Routine. Sergt Band return Jumlac. Passé men pass 152 cases through Champcleg shed	
	28/3/17	AM	Routine Visit all units under Vets Chge. examine for "Somalli Carby viva" Routine Sanitary section to 130 471 heavy Battenii attend conference ADVS. inoc 14 Corps Cpls.	

J.G.Brown

WAR DIARY or INTELLIGENCE SUMMARY

Army Form C. 2118

48th Mobile Veterinary Section

Instructions regarding War Diaries and Intelligence Summaries are contained in F. S. Regs., Part II. and the Staff Manual respectively. Title Pages will be prepared in manuscript.

(Erase heading not required.)

Place	Date	Hour	Summary of Events and Information	Remarks and references to Appendices
BAILLEUL	1/3/17	AM	Routine. Pass 66 cases through champeting shed. Dispose of three unserviceable horses to brecknels for F150, M5, V50	
		PM	Routine. Visit 14 Corps trop.	
	2/3/17	AM	Routine. 124 cases through champeting shed. Disposed of sick animals under Vety charge unfit for brecknels.	all ams under Vety charge unfit for breckth. to 23 V.H.
		PM	Routine. General Nugent 36 Irish Commander visited surgeon section. 2 + 43 are cases	
	3/3/17	AM	General "General Godley" visited section. attended conference ADVS re Reun fitzgeruld tokens to indent.	
		PM	Routine. visit Col PALMER. DDVS. 2"ARMY. re supplies received in Ind units.	
	4/3/17	AM	Routine. Dispatched 2 sich cases by motor Ambulance to 23 Vety Hospital	
		PM	Routine. visited suspected 2" Anzac HQrs + all animals for strath. Culagence.	
	5/3/17	AM	Routine. Pass 175. horses through champeting shed.	
		PM	Routine. Visit surgeful all units under Vety Charge for stratith Contagiosa	
	6/3/17	AM	Routine. Visit 14 Corps troops force 172 animals through champeting shed turne in new Brosana from Ambulance from 5 Vety Hospital. Paid men	
		PM	Routine. ams visits section. Dispatch 32 cases to 23 VETY. HOSP.: by motor & 6 cases through champeting shed	Paid men. by train. Paso 171 through champeting shed

Army Form C. 2118

WAR DIARY
or
INTELLIGENCE SUMMARY
(Erase heading not required.)

Instructions regarding War Diaries and Intelligence Summaries are contained in F.S. Regs., Part II. and the Staff Manual respectively. Title Pages will be prepared in manuscript.

Place	Date	Hour	Summary of Events and Information	Remarks and references to Appendices
Ballrul	7/3/17	A.M	Routine despatch 21 animals to Field Remount Section Hazebrouck. 2 returned.	
		P.M.	Routine Pass 163 animals through disinfecting shed.	
	8/3/17	A.M.	Routine Visit Hqrs. Bde. & 6th Fd. Co.	
		P.M.	Routine Pass animals through disinfecting shed	
	9/3/17	A.M	Routine Forced in 10 days. Special leave animals 10 ind.	
		P.M	Took over Capt Clowes duties, inspected at M.V.S. Routine	Proposed to increase leave to Dec Shop for Ft 200/-
	10/3/17	A.M	Routine Visited H.Q. Qr. & New Sig. Coy. inspected at M.V.S. Ft. 200/-	
		P.M	Routine	
	11/3/17	A.M	Inspected 2nd Anzac H.Q. Qr. Horses. Saw Certificate for 2/6 60/25	
			Remounts	
		P.M	Routine	
	12/3/17	A.M	Drew Ft.500/- from Field Cashier. Payment of Section attached	
		P.M	Routine	
	13/3/17	A.M	Inspected 16 Horses proceeding by barge. Routine	
		P.M	Routine	
	14/3/17	A.M	Visited M.V.S. inspected. Routine	
		P.M		

WAR DIARY
or
INTELLIGENCE SUMMARY
(Erase heading not required.)

Army Form C. 2118

Instructions regarding War Diaries and Intelligence Summaries are contained in F.S. Regs., Part II. and the Staff Manual respectively. Title Pages will be prepared in manuscript.

Place	Date	Hour	Summary of Events and Information	Remarks and references to Appendices
	15/3/17	Am	Routine	
		Pm	Routine	
	16/3/17	Am	Mated Sect. inspected & arrangers for camp Par stores Routine	
		Pm	Visited HQ Ars & Sis Coy R.E.	
	17/3/17		Routine	
		Am	Routine. Visited Div Sig Coy R.E.	
		Pm	Routine. To fall of movements since 1/175	
	18/3/17	Am	Routine	
		Pm	Routine. Inspected M.T. arranged for horses to St Stephen annexes	
	19/3/17	Noon	Routine By road etc.	
		Pm	Routine St Stephen annexes etc. 9 animals evacuated by barge	
	20/3/17	Am	Routine	
		8 pm	Routine "Fall of movements since few	
	21/3/17	Am	Routine. Return for Reeve Stan in Club at M.S.	
		P.M.	Routine. Visit newspod. 10 g. Field Ambulance. Sergt. Schofield proceed on 10 day's leave	
	22/3/17	AM	Routine. Paid men.	
		P.M.	received ... draw of 600 from Field Cashier	

Army Form C. 2118

WAR DIARY
or
INTELLIGENCE SUMMARY
(Erase heading not required.)

Instructions regarding War Diaries and Intelligence Summaries are contained in F. S. Regs., Part II. and the Staff Manual respectively. Title Pages will be prepared in manuscript.

Place	Date	Hour	Summary of Events and Information	Remarks and references to Appendices
BAILLEUL	23/3/17	A.M.	Routine. Visit outpost 2nd HQrs. HQR RA PRE Visits Hosp to lecture to nurses.	
		P.M.	Routine. Attend Conference ADMS Office.	
HODGE MACKER	24/3/17	A.M.	Move to HODGE-MACKER. Staff up Standing sub 86 Inf. TRAIN.	
		P.M.	Visit 23 Vety. Hospital well ADMS.	
	25/3/17	A.M.	Routine. ADMS visits actions.	
		P.M.	Routine.	
	26/3/17	A.M.	Routine. Visit ouspots. 2nd HQRs HQRA, RE, 2nd 2 Lt Co RE	
		P.M.	Routine. Visit 108, 109 FIELD AMBULANCES. Inspect of mewrable horse 6 Rechterie Baillad for. F.co 175.—	
	27/3/17	A.M.	Routine. ADMS visits actions. Inspect 14 cases by rail & 88 6 horse & 23 VM.	
		P.M.	Routine. Obtain materials from CRE for bullery stalls etc	
	28/3/17	A.M.	Routine.	
		P.M.	Routine.	
	29/3/17	A.M.	Routine. Visit 10 9 FIELD Ambulance	
		P.M.	Routine. Visit Zulu Kennel Section Ingleinek	

A. Gough.

Army Form C. 2118

WAR DIARY
or
INTELLIGENCE SUMMARY

(Erase heading not required.)

Instructions regarding War Diaries and Intelligence Summaries are contained in F. S. Regs., Part II. and the Staff Manual respectively. Title Pages will be prepared in manuscript.

Place	Date	Hour	Summary of Events and Information	Remarks and references to Appendices
BAPAUME	30/3/17	A.M.	Routine. Report 8 cases to 23 Vety. Hospital. ADVS not seen.	
		P.M.	Routine. Conference D.D.V.S. Office	
	31/3/17	A.M.	Routine. Visit - 108 Field Ambulance	
		P.M	Routine. Pass animals through 14 Corps Horse. D.I.P.	J.H.Ross

Army Form C. 2118

45th Mobile Vet. Section

WAR DIARY
or
INTELLIGENCE SUMMARY
(Erase heading not required.)

Instructions regarding War Diaries and Intelligence Summaries are contained in F.S. Regs., Part II. and the Staff Manual respectively. Title Pages will be prepared in manuscript.

Place	Date	Hour	Summary of Events and Information	Remarks and references to Appendices
MOOSE MAGE	1/4/17	A.M.	Routine Visit EN SAD S.	
		P.M.	Routine ADVS med section	
	2/4/17	A.M.	Routine Visit sick horses. HQ's RATE Cav Bde Cav Div.	
		P.M.	Routine Visit No 109 Field Amb. 3 cases turned in for knee	
			had found to be cured report A.D.M.S. 36 Div.	
	3/4/17	A.M.	Routine Inspect 3 sick animals L B Vety Hospital 3 horses from	
			WOODEN HORSE	
		P.M.	Routine Inspect 8 horse hutts to be bar by Army form it came horse guns	
	4/4/17	A.M.	Routine A.D.V.S. med section.	
		P.M.	Routine Visit DECHILDRE BAILLEUL	
	5/4/17	A.M.	Routine Visit & inspect all sick under Vety. charge	
		P.M.	Routine Serg't SCHOFIELD returns from leave.	
	6/4/17	A.M.	Routine Inspect 13 sick animals L B VETY HOSPITAL 11 horses	
		P.M.		

1875 Wt. W593/826 1,000,000 4/15 J.B.C. & A. A.D.S.S./Forms/C. 2118.

WAR DIARY
or
INTELLIGENCE SUMMARY

(Erase heading not required.)

Army Form C. 2118

Place	Date	Hour	Summary of Events and Information	Remarks and references to Appendices
Rood House	7/4/17 AM	Writing	Pay'g rich other than 4500 from Field Cashier	
	P.M.	Routine	Sending asten to 72 Co. R.F.A. Pay men	
	8/4/17 AM	Routine	Visit Post HBK. Hurr. MAKE. 17th SIG. CoY.	
	P.M.	Routine	Visit to 109 Field Ambulances	
	9/4/17 P.M.	Routine		
	P.M.	Routine		
	10/4/17 P.M.	Routine	Visit all unit untel 157% charge dispatch 7 set animals also to 23A.H.	
	P.M.	Routine	Visit Col Palmer, 2 D.M. & Charges for last fort	
	11/4/17 P.M.	Routine	Sending victim to 181 GFA	
	P.M.	Routine	men to Baths	
	12/4/17 AM	Routine	Hoof Brigad all uned under Vety charge	
	P.M.	Routine		
	13/4/17 AM	Routine	Visit Div H.Qu.	
	P.M.	Writing	Around Confidential Reports Ryes	

WAR DIARY or INTELLIGENCE SUMMARY

Army Form C. 2118

(Erase heading not required.)

Instructions regarding War Diaries and Intelligence Summaries are contained in F. S. Regs., Part II. and the Staff Manual respectively. Title Pages will be prepared in manuscript.

Place	Date	Hour	Summary of Events and Information	Remarks and references to Appendices
HOOGSTRAETEN	13/7/17	A.M.	Routine. Had transport unit with Vety Corporal	
		P.M.	Routine. Inspection of mismarnails. Knot to substitute for #175	
	15/7/17	A.M.	Routine. Inspection of remounts prior to being sent on. Some compresses	
		P.M.	Routine.	
	16/7/17	A.M.	Routine. Visit & inspect Sub. Hqrs. 110th R.E., R.A. & 5th V.C. Coy.	
		P.M.	Routine. Insp. & inspect 108 & 109 Field Ambulances	
	17/7/17	A.M.	Routine. Inspected 10 sick animals & began to substitute for 21 NCY horses/mules	
			9 & 2 by road.	
		P.M.	Routine. Inspection of mismarnails prior to substitute for #175	
	18/7/17	A.M.	Routine. Visit all units under Vety charge	
		P.M.	Routine. Recommend Cpl. WRIGHT for a commission	
	19/7/17	A.M.	Routine	
		P.M.	Routine	

WAR DIARY
or
INTELLIGENCE SUMMARY

(Erase heading not required.)

Army Form C. 2118

Instructions regarding War Diaries and Intelligence Summaries are contained in F. S. Regs., Part II. and the Staff Manual respectively. Title Pages will be prepared in manuscript.

Place	Date	Hour	Summary of Events and Information	Remarks and references to Appendices
Rouen	20/4/17	PM		
Rouen	21/4/17	AM	Attended Conference Eng Base	
Rouen		PM	Pay room	
Rouen	22/4/17	AM	Let work.	
Rouen		PM		
Rouen	23/4/17	PM		
Rouen	24/4/17	AM	Visit to Hqrs Dir SS&T, AD Med CCRA	
Rouen		PM	Visit 10th, 11th Field Ambulances	
Rouen	25/4/17	AM	Visits - Sickr Horse Kman Gen Bar Horse Shows	
Rouen		PM		
Rouen	26/4/17	AM		
Rouen		PM		
Rouen	27/4/17	PM	Visit Transport Hqt 11½ Div	
Rouen		PM	" 10th, 11th Field Ambulances	

Army Form C. 2118

WAR DIARY
or
INTELLIGENCE SUMMARY
(Erase heading not required.)

Instructions regarding War Diaries and Intelligence Summaries are contained in F.S. Regs., Part II. and the Staff Manual respectively. Title Pages will be prepared in manuscript.

Place	Date	Hour	Summary of Events and Information	Remarks and references to Appendices
Hoogstadt	27/4/17	AM	Rostine. Reported 2 cases of dogs to 23 V.Sy. No 3 Pet Al.	
	27/4/17	PM	Routine. Inspected NCO & men who to cases changer IC and harness absent inspection 2045 from.	
	28/4/17	AM	Routine. NCO & 6 men took sir baths	
		PM	Routine	
	29/4/17	AM	Routine. Church service for men	
		PM	Routine	
	30/4/17	AM	Routine. Had A.C. much medic Corp Large	
		PM	Routine	

1875 Wt. W593/826 1,000,000 4/15 J.B.C. & A. A.D.S.S./Forms/C. 2118.

Army Form C. 2118

WAR DIARY
or
INTELLIGENCE SUMMARY 48th Mobile Veterinary Section

(Erase heading not required.)

Place	Date	Hour	Summary of Events and Information	Remarks and references to Appendices
HODGENACKER	1/5/17	AM	Routine Despatch 3 sick animals to 23 V.H.	
		P.M.	Routine. Take in 19 Cavy Bake	
	2/5/17	AM	Routine Visit stripped 150 Field GRF	
		P.M.	Routine	
	3/5/17	AM	Routine Visit stripped all und under VS charge	
		PM	Routine	
	4/5/17	AM	Routine Beyond Steen annex by layer 42204	
		PM	Routine attend Expense Advs office.	
	5/5/17	AM	Routine Sanitary Lectr to 13 R.R.	
		PM	Routine Visit General Corks Horse	
	6/5/17	AM	Routine Ray men.	
		PM	Routines	
	7/5/17	AM	Routine Inattendance 76 "But Horse Show.	
		PM	Routine	

Army Form C. 2118

WAR DIARY
or
INTELLIGENCE SUMMARY
(Erase heading not required.)

*Instructions regarding War Diaries and Intelligence Summaries are contained in F. S. Regs., Part II. and the Staff Manual respectively. Title Pages will be prepared in manuscript.

Place	Date	Hour	Summary of Events and Information	Remarks and references to Appendices
Rouen	8/5/17	AM	Routine. Visit of inspect: Ind. HQrs, HQrs RA, RE, 17th Bn Sig. Co RE	
	8/5/17	PM	Routine. Visit of inspect to 108 & 109 Field Ambulances	
	9/5/17	AM	Routine. Dispatch cases to 23 Vety. Hospital	
	9/5/17	PM	Routine. Paid men of A.V.S. Staff. Drill order.	
	10/5/17	AM	Routine. Visit all and under Vety. charge	
	10/5/17	PM	Routine. Inspection of manure to Isolated Paddock no. 175	
	11/5/17	AM	Routine. Attended conference A.D.V.S office	
	11/5/17	PM	Routine. Dispatch 4 cases to 23 Vety. Hospital BFF & FTR	
	12/5/17	AM	Routine. Jan in Vety. Charge of 285 A.T. Co R.E	
	12/5/17	PM	Routine. Collect 1 Raises from FLD. REM. SEC.	
	13/5/17	AM	Routine. A.V.S. mail. Return.	
	13/5/17	PM	Routine.	
	14/5/17	AM	Routine. Visit all and under Vety. Charge	
	14/5/17	PM		

WAR DIARY
or
INTELLIGENCE SUMMARY
(Erase heading not required.)

Army Form C. 2118

Instructions regarding War Diaries and Intelligence Summaries are contained in F. S. Regs., Part II. and the Staff Manual respectively. Title Pages will be prepared in manuscript.

Place	Date	Hour	Summary of Events and Information	Remarks and references to Appendices
HOOGEWACKER	15/5/17	AM	Routine. Inspect 285 A.T. Co RE	
		PM	Routine. Despatch Cases to 23 Vety. Hospital.	
	16/5/17	AM	Routine. Drill order. Box respirator drill	
		PM	Routine	
	17/5/17	AM	Routine. Visit inspect all units under Vety. Charge	
		PM	Routine	
	18/5/17	AM	Routine. Despatch 12 cases to 23 Vety. Hospital attend conference ADVS Ypres.	
		P.M.	Routine. Visit Inspect 285 A.T. Co RE	
	19/5/17	A.M.	Routine	
		P.M.	Routine.	
	20/5/17	AM	Routine. Pte Checkley 13972. Granted leave 10 days exp.	
		P.M.	Routine	
	21/5/17	AM	Routine. Visit inspect all units under Vety. Charge. Draw £500 for Field Cashier	
		PM	Routine. Pay men	
	22/5/17	AM	Routine. Despatch 5 Cases to 23 Vety Hospital	
		P.M.		

OFFICER COMMANDING
No.
Date No 17
#184 MOBILE VETERINARY

WAR DIARY or INTELLIGENCE SUMMARY

Army Form C. 2118

Place	Date	Hour	Summary of Events and Information	Remarks and references to Appendices
HOOGENACKER	23/5/17	A.M.	Routine ADVS work section	
		P.M.	Routine	
	24/5/17	A.M.	Routine Visit to HQrs, HQ R, RE Fut L, C	
		P.M.	Routine Visit Field Ambulances	
	25/5/17	AM	Routine attend Conference ADVS 7gne evacuate S.Cases to 23 VH. L	
		PM	Routine	
	26/5/17	AM	Routine Vad units	
		PM	Routine dispose of 1 incurable horse to DESCHILDRE	
	27/5/17	AM	Routine front to evacuate camp beginning on to Shelling 10.35 pm 6 9 am	
		PM	Routine	
	28/5/17	AM	Routine Vad all units under Veg charge. Chanelle 2 Styphd	
		PM	Routine again shelled out of camp between 12-20 to 3-30 AM AM	
	29/5/17	AM	Routine send 5 case to 23 Vety Hospital	
		PM	Routine	

Army Form C. 2118

WAR DIARY
or
INTELLIGENCE SUMMARY
(Erase heading not required.)

Place	Date	Hour	Summary of Events and Information	Remarks and references to Appendices
HOOGENACKER	30/5/17	AM	Routine disposal of 1 inserviceable horse to DESCHILD RE	
		PM	Routine	
	31/5/17	AM	Routine. Evacuate 51 cases by road & 18 by canal to 23 Vet HOSPITAL.	
		PM	Routine visit & inspect all units under Very. Charge D.D.V.S. not action	

48th Mobile Veterinary Section

WAR DIARY
or
INTELLIGENCE SUMMARY.
(Erase heading not required.)

Army Form C. 2118.

Instructions regarding War Diaries and Intelligence Summaries are contained in F. S. Regs., Part II. and the Staff Manual respectively. Title pages will be prepared in manuscript.

Vol 21

Place	Date	Hour	Summary of Events and Information	Remarks and references to Appendices
HOOGENACKER	1/6/17	AM	Routine.	
		PM	Routine. attend conference ADVS Office	
	2/6/17	AM	Routine DDVS. visit section	
		PM.	Routine	
	3/6/17	AM	Routine Visit all unit under Vety Charge	
		PM	Routine	
	4/6/17	AM	Routine ADVS visit section	
		PM	Routine visit unit	
	5/6/17	AM	Routine evacuate 20 Cases to 23 Vety. HOSPITAL	
		PM	Routine	
	6/6/17	AM	Routine Throw out ADVANCED VET. AID Pat at ORANOUTRE	
		PM	Routine	
	7/6/17	AM	Routine In attendance at A.V.A.P.	
		PM	Routine do	
	8/6/17	AM	Routine In attendance at AVAP	
		PM	Routine attend conference ADVS Office	

Army Form C. 2118.

WAR DIARY
or
INTELLIGENCE SUMMARY.
(Erase heading not required.)

Place	Date	Hour	Summary of Events and Information	Remarks and references to Appendices
HOOGENACKER	9/6/17	AM	Routine. Inattendance at S.V.A.P.	
		PM	Routine. Visit all units.	
St. JANS CAPPEL	10/6/17	AM	Routine. hurr section to St Jans CAPPEL	
		PM	Routine	
	11/6/17	AM	Routine ASVS roll section	
		PM	Routine. Visit units	
	12/6/17	AM	Routine. Evacuate 14 cases by road to 2.3 V.H.	
		PM	Routine	
	13/6/17	AM	Routine. Visit units. Draw £500 from Field Cashier	
		PM	Routine. Pay men	
	14/6/17	AM	Routine. ASVS proceed on leave. Relieved Sub'n J. Lamb	
		PM	Routine. evacuate 2 cases by motor ambulance	
	15/6/17	AM	Routine. Sent his cases by motor ambulance	
		PM	Routine. Sent. 6 cases to I.K CORPS. M.V.D. Preside at conference ASVS	
	16/6/17	AM	Routine. Visit units	
		PM	Routine	

Army Form C. 2118.

WAR DIARY
or
INTELLIGENCE SUMMARY.
(Erase heading not required.)

Instructions regarding War Diaries and Intelligence Summaries are contained in F. S. Regs., Part II. and the Staff Manual respectively. Title pages will be prepared in manuscript.

Place	Date	Hour	Summary of Events and Information	Remarks and references to Appendices
St JANS CAPEL	17/6/17	AM	Routine ADVS 19th Div" visit section.	
		PM	Routine evacuated 6 animals to 17 Corps MVD	
	18/6/17	AM	Routine. Visit unit	
		P.M.	Routine 2 animals evacuated by Motor Ambulance	
	19/6/17	AM	Routine move section to Locre M.23, Central MAP 27. Shave over from 19th Bret MVS	
		PM	Routine take over 21 Cases from 11th Bret MVS	
	20/6/17	AM	Routine evacuate 20 cases by road to 23 VH?	
		PM	Routine pay men	
	21/6/17	AM	Routine Visit surgical unit	
		PM	Routine	
	22/6/17	AM	Routine	
		PM	Routine Proceed at Conference ADVS Office	
	23/6/17	AM	Routine Visit units.	
		PM	Routine Saw field from Kuchelm	
	24/6/17	AM	Routine visit 109 Field Ambulance	
		PM	Routine Church Parade for men	

T2134. Wt. W708-776. 500000. 4/15. Sir J. C. & S.

Army Form C. 2118.

WAR DIARY
or
INTELLIGENCE SUMMARY.
(Erase heading not required.)

Place	Date	Hour	Summary of Events and Information	Remarks and references to Appendices
LOCRE	25/6/17	AM	Routine Visit all units	
		PM	Routine Drew £250 from Field Cashier IX Corps	
	26/6/17	AM	Routine ADVS return from leave	
		PM	Routine Land over charge	
	27/6/17	AM	Routine DDVS visit section	
		PM	Routine Jump horse at 23rd Mob. Horse Stores	
	28/6/17	AM	Routine Visit all units. Evacuate 41 Cases by road to 23 Vety. Hospital	
		PM	Routine Evacuate 24 Cases to IX Corps, M.V.D.	
	29/4/17	AM	Routine Evacuate 6 Cases to MVD	
		PM	Routine Visit units. Attend conference ADVS Office	
	30/6/17	AM	Routine Horse to new area	
		PM	Routine "	
	1/7/17	AM	Routine	
		PM		

Army Form C. 2118.

WAR DIARY
or
INTELLIGENCE SUMMARY.
(Erase heading not required.)

Mob Vet Sec
Vol 22

Place	Date	Hour	Summary of Events and Information	Remarks and references to Appendices
MERRIS	1/7/17	AM	Routine - Church parade	
		PM	Routine	
	2/7/17	AM	Routine - Visit 108 & 109 Field Ambulances	
		PM	Routine - Visit 108 Field Ambulance. Sent for two cases littoral N.C. 8.5.5.	
	3/7/17	AM	Routine ASC mails return	
		PM	Routine Draw £500 from Field Cashier	
	4/7/17	AM	Routine Pay man.	
		PM	Routine Bath for men.	
	5/7/17	AM	Routine Evacuate 10 animals to M Corps M.V.D.	
HONDEGEM		PM	Move to HONDEGEM. Sub area incl 109 Inf Bn. Inspected by G.O.C 109 Bn.	
ARQUES	6/7/17	AM	Move to Arques area. Inspected by G.O.C 108 Inf Bde	
		PM		
ZUDAUSQUES	7/7/17	AM	Move to ZUDAUSQUES area attached 108 Inf Bde	
		PM		
ACQUIN	8/7/17	AM	Move to ACQUIN attached 107 Inf Bde	
		PM		

Army Form C. 2118.

WAR DIARY
or
INTELLIGENCE SUMMARY.
(Erase heading not required.)

Instructions regarding War Diaries and Intelligence Summaries are contained in F.S. Regs., Part II. and the Staff Manual respectively. Title pages will be prepared in manuscript.

Place	Date	Hour	Summary of Events and Information	Remarks and references to Appendices
ACQUIN	9/7/17	AM	Routine. DADVS visit section. Visit 108 Inf. Bde.	
		PM	Routine. Jake over duties of Capt. Millar A.V.C. proceeding on leave.	
	10/7/17	AM	Routine. Visit & inspect all units. 109 Inf. Bde.	
		PM	Routine.	
	11/7/17	AM	Visit & inspect all units 107 Inf. Bde. Routine.	
		PM	Routine.	
	12/7/17	AM	Routine. George Jumpers at Bde Sports.	
		PM	Routine.	
	13/7/17	AM	Routine. Visit all units 108 Inf. Bde. ADMS visit unpaid Pollack Stallion.	
		PM	Routine. Took over vety duties of Capt Whyte sent to base in relation in established.	
	14/7/17	AM	Routine. Visit all units 109 Inf. Bde. 78th Train.	
		PM	Routine. Dispatch animals to 23 Vety. Hospital.	
	15/7/17	AM	Routine. Visit all units 107 Inf. Bde v Div Train	
		PM	Routine.	
	16/7/17	AM	Routine. Visit all units 108 Inf. Bde	
		PM	Routine. Visit Div. Train.	

Army Form C. 2118.

WAR DIARY
or
INTELLIGENCE SUMMARY.
(Erase heading not required.)

Instructions regarding War Diaries and Intelligence Summaries are contained in F. S. Regs., Part II. and the Staff Manual respectively. Title pages will be prepared in manuscript.

Place	Date	Hour	Summary of Events and Information	Remarks and references to Appendices
ACQUIN	17/7/17	AM	Routine Visit all units 109 INF BDE	
		PM	Routine Visit DIV. TRAIN. ADVS visits return	
	18/7/17	AM	Routine Visit inspect all units 107 INF BDE	
		PM	Routine Visit inspect DIV TRAIN	
	19/7/17	AM	Routine Visit inspect all units 108 INF BDE	
		PM	Routine Visit inspect DIV TRAIN	
	20/7/17	AM	Routine Visit-s inspect 109 INF. BDE. Drew £500 from FIELD CASHIER St. OMER	
		PM	Routine Visit inspect DIV TRAIN Pay him ADVS visit return	
	21/7/17	AM	Routine Visit inspect 107 BDE.	
		PM	Routine Visit inspect 3rd TRAIN	
	22/7/17	AM	Routine Gymnahana d'AQUIN. Capt. MILLAR return from leave	
		PM	Routine "	
	23/7/17	AM	Routine Visit 108 Bde	
		PM	Routine Visit inspect DIV TRAIN	
	24/7/17	AM	Routine Visit 109 FIELD AMBULANCE	
		PM	Routine	

Army Form C. 2118.

WAR DIARY
or
INTELLIGENCE SUMMARY.
(Erase heading not required.)

Instructions regarding War Diaries and Intelligence Summaries are contained in F. S. Regs., Part II. and the Staff Manual respectively. Title pages will be prepared in manuscript.

Place	Date	Hour	Summary of Events and Information	Remarks and references to Appendices
AQUIN.	25/7/17	AM	Routine Visit all units	
		PM	Routine " Ful train visit 3 Vety. Hospital Boulogne	
NOORDPEENE	26/7/17	AM	Move to NOORDPEENE	
		PM		
WINNIZEELE	27/7/17	AM	Move to WINNIZEELE	
		PM		
	28/7/17	AM	Routine Visit N°s 2,3,4 Coys train	
		PM	Routine	
	29/7/17	AM	Routine Visit 121, 122, & 150 Field Ambs	
		PM	Routine " Stfs Train	
WATOU	30/7/17	AM	Move to WATOU area L'13.b.3.4	
		PM	Pay men	
	31/7/17	AM	Vet Train Y RE's	
		PM	Routine	

WAR DIARY
or
INTELLIGENCE SUMMARY.

(Erase heading not required.)

Army Form C. 2118.

Instructions regarding War Diaries and Intelligence Summaries are contained in F. S. Regs., Part II. and the Staff Manual respectively. Title pages will be prepared in manuscript.

Place	Date	Hour	Summary of Events and Information	Remarks and references to Appendices
WATOU (Area)	1/8/17	AM	Routine. Visit all Coys Div'l TRAIN.	
		PM	Routine. Visit Field Coys. RE	
	2/8/17	AM	Routine. Visit all Coys Div'l TRAIN.	
		PM	Routine. evacuate to M.V.D. "WIPPER HOECK"	
	3/8/17	AM	Routine. Visit all Coys Div'l TRAIN	
		PM	Routine. draw £1,000 from FIELD CASHIER XIX CORPS	
	4/8/17	AM	Routine. Visit all Coys Div'l TRAIN. Visit 53rd Div'l M.V.S at G.19.4.6. S.28 N.W.	
		PM	Routine. evacuate to M.V.D XIX CORPS.	
POPERINGHE	5/8/17	AM	Move to "POPERINGHE" G.11.4.6. V take over from 53rd Div'l M.V.S.	
		PM	Visit all Coys Div'l TRAIN. 150 FIELD Co RE. Cpl BUCK Y Pte CHALKLEY take over Advanced VET. AID POST at "YPRES" Blancelli 150 RE bombs 1 mule destroyed	
	6/8/17	AM	Routine. Parade attend to 8am visit Vanguard 150, 121 V 122 FIELD Cos RE visit VET. AID Post	
		PM	Routine. DADVS visit section Joey. man visit all Coys train	
	7/8/17	AM	Routine. Visit 3 FIELD Coys. take over Vety. Charge Visit 3rd B. Reserve BTC.	
		PM	Routine. Visit advanced aid post V all Coys Div' TRAIN	
	8/8/17	AM	Routine. BTVS visit section. status not actions. Visit Field Coys. RE	
		PM	Routine. Vet. advanced aid post mule DADVS. Visit Div'l TRAIN units	

Army Form C. 2118.

WAR DIARY
or
INTELLIGENCE SUMMARY.
(Erase heading not required.)

Instructions regarding War Diaries and Intelligence Summaries are contained in F. S. Regs., Part II. and the Staff Manual respectively. Title pages will be prepared in manuscript.

A.D.V.S. VD703

Place	Date	Hour	Summary of Events and Information	Remarks and references to Appendices
POPERINGHE	9/8/17	PM	Routine. DADVS visit section & inspect 50 animals proceeding to base. Visit Vinyard.	
			2" Traffic Control Sqd. 121 v 122 Field Co. RE & 3rd Reserve BDE MGC with DADVS	
		PM	Routine. Visit advanced Vet. AID POST. Evacuate 10 cases by foot throw ambulance to M.V.D.	
	10/8/17	AM	Routine. evacuate 40 cases to XIX CORPS. M.V.D. Visit 3rd RDAC. PM on horse at 3rd RESERVE TANKS.	
			Visit ADVANCED VET. AID. POST. DADVS visits section	
		PM	Routine. Visit Vinyard. 150 RE attend conference DADVS office. ADVS visits section Pte FITZPATRICK wound	
	11/8/17	AM	Routine. Camp boarded for 2nd Visit VET AID POST. 150 FIELD CO RE DADVS visit section	
		PM	Routine. Visit all Cavy S Div "TRAIN". 121 v 122 FIELD CO RE	
	12/8/17	AM	Routine. here as "38" LABOUR GROUP. TCM on examine 22 Remounts at PROVEN.	
		PM	Routine. Visit ADVANCED VET AID POST. Visit 121 v 122 FIELD Cy. RE. 7 Au Cavy S DIV "TRAIN".	
	13/8/17	AM	Routine. ADVS XIX CORPS TDADVS visit section V Inspect. 100 carts for Evacuation to M.V.D.	
		P.M.	Visit ADVANCED VET. AID POST visit all Cavy S DIV "TRAIN" P.M. Men	
	14/8/17	AM	Routine. Exam on & Inspect 120 Remounts at PROVEN visit ADVANCED VET. AID POST.	
			Join on 66th LABOUR GROUP	
		PM	Routine. Visit all Cavy S Div "TRAIN"	
	15/8/17	AM	Routine. Visit "advanced Vet. AID. Post", 3rd RESERVE DAC. 150. RE	Chown
		PM	Routine. Visit Div. TRAIN. DADVS visits section	Chown

Army Form C. 2118.

WAR DIARY
or
INTELLIGENCE SUMMARY.
(Erase heading not required.)

Instructions regarding War Diaries and Intelligence Summaries are contained in F. S. Regs., Part II. and the Staff Manual respectively. Title pages will be prepared in manuscript.

Place	Date	Hour	Summary of Events and Information	Remarks and references to Appendices
POPERINGHE	16/8/17	AM.	Routine. Visit Advanced Vet. Aid Post. Post point on WIELTJE road Vaal 121 Y/R 2 RE	
		PM	Routine. Evacuate 60 cases to XIX Corps MVD. Visit DIV TRAIN. VISIT. MVD	
	17/8/17	AM	Routine. Visit aid post 5 patrol 3rd reserve ATC. 150 RE. 66th LABOUR Co,	
		PM	Routine. Visit DIV TRAIN. 38th LABOUR Coys. 73 LABOUR Coy.	
WINNIZEELE	18/8/17	AM	Routine. Unit move to WINNIZEELE area. Section taken over by 61 Div Mushes Section	
		PM	Evacuate 56 cases to XIX Corps MVD.	
	19/8/17	AM	Routine. Visit all Coys 1st DIV TRAIN	
		PM	Routine. Lt. McConnel sentenced 28 days FP No 1 for insolence to NCO See 150 RE	
	20/8/17	AM.	Routine. Saxie over v Archibald. 22 Remount at PROVEN.	
		PM	Routine. Visit Sergent 150 Field Co RE	
	21/8/17	AM	Routine. Visit all Coys train. Starts vail section.	
		PM	Routine. Visit 121 Field Co RE	
	22/8/17	AM	Routine. Visit all Coys train. 150 Field Co RE	
		PM	Routine. Visit 121 Field Coy RE. Iain in GSW from SRIR.	
	23/8/17	AM	Routine. Visit DIV TRAIN, Field Coys RE	
		P.M.	Routine. Take my charge 36 Div Artillery. vis Capt. McClintock on leave	G Rose [signature]

Army Form C. 2118.

WAR DIARY
or
INTELLIGENCE SUMMARY.
(Erase heading not required.)

Instructions regarding War Diaries and Intelligence Summaries are contained in F. S. Regs., Part II. and the Staff Manual respectively. Title pages will be prepared in manuscript.

A.D.V.S.
P+ VD703
SEP 17
ULSTER DIVISION

Place	Date	Hour	Summary of Events and Information	Remarks and references to Appendices
WINNIZEELE (area)	24/8/17	A.M.	Visit A,B,D Batteries 173 RFA. Routine hit ADVS XIT CORPS re debility cant D173	
		P.M.	Routine Visit B 153 RFA.	
	25/8/17	A.M.	Routine evacuate 20 Cooks to XIT CORPS M.V.D.	
		PM	Routine visit r inspect No 1 (HQ) Coy 36 Dn TRN.	
	26/8/17	AM	Routine visit r inspect HQ. R.A. A, B. 173 BDE. RFA	
		PM	Routine. visit r inspect Bt D 153 Bde RFA. C r D 173 Bde RFA.	
	27/8/17	AM	Routine. visit r inspect C r E Battys. 153 BDE RFA.	
		PM	Routine. visit No. 1 (HQ) Coy 36 DIV.TRN.	
	28/8/17		Entrained at CASSEL STATION. 9.41 PM.	
	29/8/17		arrived BAPAUME. 9-0 AM. proceed to ETRICOURT. admitted to 31. CCS with a SEPTIC HAND.	H Oulart [?]
ETRICOURT	30/8/17		ADVS IV CORPS. DADVS 36 DIVISION visits section	
do	31/8/17		SECTION administered temporarily by ADVS 36 Division	

WAR DIARY
or
INTELLIGENCE SUMMARY.
(Erase heading not required.)

Army Form C. 2118.

Instructions regarding War Diaries and Intelligence Summaries are contained in F. S. Regs., Part II. and the Staff Manual respectively. Title pages will be prepared in manuscript.

Place	Date	Hour	Summary of Events and Information	Remarks and references to Appendices
ETRICOURT	1/9/17	AM	Routine. ADVS IV Corps & RADVS 36 DIVISION visits section	
— do —		PM	Routine	
— do —	2/9/17	AM	Routine DADVS 36 DIVISION visits section	
— do —		PM	Routine	
— do —	3/9/17	AM	Routine ADVS IV CORP - DADVS 36 DIVISION visits section Brewjean H.P Cochier	
— do —		PM	Routine Bathing parade for men at 21 CCS. Paid men	
— do —	4/9/17	AM	Routine Evacuate 10 Horses & 15 mules to N° 7 VETY HOSPITAL FORGES LES EAUX.	
— do —		PM	Routine T4/44580 Pt GORDON R granted 10 days leave.	
— do —	5/9/17	AM	Routine R.A.D V.S. 36 DIVISION visits section.	
— do —		PM	Routine. Bathing parade for men at 2.6.6.5. ADVS IV CORPS visits section	
— do —	6/9/17	AM	Routine sent float to 14th RES PARK. IV CORPS. for injured horse	
— do —		PM	Routine A.D.V.S IV CORPS visits section.	
— do —	7/9/17	AM	Routine Proceed on 10 days leave to ENGLAND.	
— do —		PM	Routine MAJOR A L HORNER DADVS 36 DIVISION takes charge	
— do —	8/9/17	AM	Routine D.A.D.V.S visits section	
— do —		PM	Routine erect NISSEN HUT from RE Dump	

WAR DIARY
or
INTELLIGENCE SUMMARY.
(Erase heading not required.)

Army Form C. 2118.

Place	Date	Hour	Summary of Events and Information	Remarks and references to Appendices
FRICOURT	9/9/17	AM	Routine. Spare Armshing hut from R.E. Dump. DADVS visits section	
		PM	Routine. ADVS IV Corps visits section	
- do -	10/9/17	AM	Routine. DADVS. visits section. Paid men.	
		PM	Routine. Bathing parade for 13 men at 21. G.C.S.	
- do -	11/9/17	AM	Routine. Evacuated 19 Horses & 3 mules by train to No.7. VETY. HOSP.	
		PM	Routine. D.A.D.V.S. 36 Division visits section.	
- do -	12/9/17	AM	Routine. Mares of 48 M.V.S. examined at 36 Div A? QMS	
		PM	Routine. Bathing parade for 10 men at 21. C.C.S.	
- do -	13/9/17	AM	Routine. No. 108399 Pte Button J. ASC from No.1 (HQ) Coy. ASC.	
		PM	Routine. ADVS IV CORPS & DDVS 3rd Army visits section	
do	14/9/17	AM	Routine. DADVS 36 Divn visits section	
		PM	Routine. DADVS. 36 Div visits section	
- do -	15/9/17	AM	Routine. DADVS 36 Div visits section	
		PM	Routine. AA & QMG & CRE visit section	
- do -	16/9/17	AM	Routine. DADVS 36 Div visits section	
		PM	Routine.	

Army Form C. 2118.

WAR DIARY
or
INTELLIGENCE SUMMARY.
(Erase heading not required.)

Instructions regarding War Diaries and Intelligence Summaries are contained in F.S. Regs., Part II. and the Staff Manual respectively. Title pages will be prepared in manuscript.

Place	Date	Hour	Summary of Events and Information	Remarks and references to Appendices
ETRICOURT	17/9/17	AM	Routine new parade for taking at 2166.S.	
do		PM	Routine. DADVS 36 Div visits section. Saw new	
do	18/9/17	AM	Routine. evacuate 22 animals by train to No 7 VET.HOSP.	
do		PM	Routine. DADVS 36 DIV visits section	
do	19/9/17	AM	Routine. DADVS 36 DIV ADVS IV CORPS visits section	
do		PM	Routine. new parade for taking at 21CCS	
do	20/9/17	AM	Routine. DADVS visits section	
do		PM	Routine. CAPT CHOWN arrives from leave.	
do	21/9/17	AM	Routine. inspection of mares for breeding purposes by	
do		AM	ADVS IV CORPS & DADVS 36 Div	
do		PM	Routine	
do	22/9/17	AM	Routine. evacuate 22 sick animals to 7 VET HOS. visit & inspect units under bty charge	
do		PM	Routine	
do	23/9/17	AM	Routine. visit & inspect units under bty charge	
do		PM	Routine	
do	24/9/17	AM	Routine. visit fri A. Dvs	
do		PM	Routine. DADVS visits section	

Army Form C. 2118.

WAR DIARY
or
INTELLIGENCE SUMMARY.
(Erase heading not required.)

Instructions regarding War Diaries and Intelligence Summaries are contained in F. S. Regs., Part II. and the Staff Manual respectively. Title pages will be prepared in manuscript.

Place	Date	Hour	Summary of Events and Information	Remarks and references to Appendices
ETRICOURT	25/9/17	AM	Routine. visit & inspect N.T. Oto. evacuate 14 animals to V/letter	
"		PM	Routine. Draw 600 frames from FIELD CASHIER. Paid men	
do	26/9/17	AM	Routine. visit A.V.Oto.	
		PM	Routine. men present at SCCS for taking	
do	27/9/17	AM	Routine. visit & inspect units under vety charge	
		PM	Routine. BADVS visits Section	
do	28/9/17	AM	Routine. Pte BOWDEN proceeds on leave	
		PM	Routine. DADVS 36 Division visits Section	
do	29/9/17	AM	Routine. evacuate to animals per train to No 7. VET.HOSPITAL	
		PM	Routine.	
do	30/9/17	A.M.	Routine. visit & inspect units under vety charge	
		PM	Routine. Cpl BUCK proceeds on leave.	

WAR DIARY or INTELLIGENCE SUMMARY

Army Form C. 2118

Place	Date	Hour	Summary of Events and Information	References to Appendices
ETRICOURT	1/10/17	AM	Routine. Visit & inspect D.H.Q. Div. Sig. Coy. RE. RA. Cpl BUCK granted leave	
		PM	Routine. Baths for men at 21.C.C.S. Paid men	
do	2/10/17	AM	Routine. Evacuate 28 animals to 7. VET. HOSPITAL.	
		PM	Routine. visit D.H.Q.	
do	3/10/17	AM	Routine. DADVS visit section	
		PM	Routine. CPL IRELAND granted leave.	
do	4/10/17	AM	Routine. visit & inspect 121 Fld Coy. RE.	
		PM	Routine. DADVS 36 Div visits section	
do	5/10/17	AM	Routine. visit & inspect D.H.Q. Div. Sig. Co. RE. RA. MMP. horses	
		PM	Routine. TAKE OVER duties of DADVS. 3 animals evacuated to No 7. VETY. HOSPITAL. by train	
do	6/10/17	AM	Routine. A.D.V.S. IV CORPS visits section	
		PM	Routine. 10885 Pte KNIGHT reverts on leave	
do	9/6/17	AM	Routine. 13 men parade for Baking at S.C.C.S.	
		PM	Routine. Paid men.	

WAR DIARY
or
INTELLIGENCE SUMMARY

(Erase heading not required.)

Army Form C.2118.

Place	Date	Hour	Summary of Events and Information	Remarks and references to Appendices
FRICOURT	9/10/17	AM	Routine visit Tangbeck until under vety charge.	
		PM	Routine	
	10/10/17	AM	Routine visit Jn. Hos Q.S	
		PM	Routine Baths to men at 21 CCS	
	11/10/17	AM	Routine visit v inspect all units under vety charge	
		PM	Routine. ADVS IV Corps visit Section	
	12/10/17	AM	Routine	
		PM	Routine ADVS IV Corps visit Section	
	13/10/17	AM	Routine. 6 animals Evacuated to 6 M.V.S. Labsil.	
		PM	Routine. 4 new & 2 men seconded from 24th & 1/60 respectively	
	14/10/17	AM	Routine. 6 men deputed to 2 VETY HOSPITAL.	
		PM	Routine. visit 6A 9V.S. OFFICE 36 DIVISION	
	15/10/17	AM	Routine visit & inspect units under vet charge. Trans stop rec'd FD CAS H/QR	
		PM	Routine one place allotted for AMIENS leave Corps Pr & men	
	16/10/17	AM	Routine 9 men received from No L VETY HOSPITAL	
		PM	Routine dispatch 15 animals to 1 VETY HOSPITAL	[signature]

WAR DIARY
or
INTELLIGENCE SUMMARY.
(Erase heading not required.)

Place	Date	Hour	Summary of Events and Information	Remarks and references to Appendices
ETRICOURT	17/10/17	AM	Routine. dispatch 1 Cpl & 5 men to No 2 VETY HOSPITAL	
do	18/10/17	PM	Routine. Baths for men at 21 CCS.	
do	18/10/17	AM	Routine. ADVS IV Corps visits section.	
		PM.	Routine.	
do	19/10/17	AM	Routine. visit & inspect SH Bty, RE, RA.	
		PM	Routine. DADVS visits section.	
do	20/10/17	AM	Routine. visit & inspect 131 Fld Co R.E. PTE KNIGHT No 10685 annon from leave	
		PM	Routine.	
do	21/10/17	AM	Routine. visit & inspect MMP. 36 Dn Sig Co RE.	
		PM	Routine.	
do	22/10/17	AM	Routine. visit 36 DHQRS.	
		PM	Routine. Baths for men at 21 CCS.	
do	23/10/17	AM	Routine. ADVS IV Corps visits section.	
		PM	Routine. evacuate 10 animals to No 7 VETY HOSP	
do	24/10/17	AM	Routine. Baths for men at 21 CCS.	
		PM	Routine. join men. American Officer inspects section.	

WAR DIARY
or
INTELLIGENCE SUMMARY.
(Erase heading not required.)

Place	Date	Hour	Summary of Events and Information	Remarks and references to Appendices
ETRICOURT	25/10/17	AM	Routine. DADVS 36 Div visits Section.	
		PM	Routine. Draws 500 francs from FIELD CASHIER.	
do	26/10/17	AM	Routine. No 6900 Pte WATMORE returns from leave.	
		PM	Routine. visit & inspect S.H. Ors.	
do	27/10/17	AM	Routine. No 6900 Pte WATMORE despatched to No 7 VETY HOSP.	
		PM	Routine. visit & inspect 121 Fld. Coy RE.	
do	28/10/17	AM	Routine. Section inspected by D.V.S. B.E.F., DDVS 3rd Army, ADVS IV Corps DADVS 36 Div	
		PM	Routine. Church parade at 2/6 GS	
do	29/10/17	AM	Routine. Baths to men at 21 CCS.	
		PM	Routine. visit & inspect mule units Vet's charge.	
do	30/10/17	AM	Routine. evacuation to No 7 VET HOSP. 1st animal per train	
		PM	Routine. visit & inspect mule units Vet's charge	
do	31/10/17	AM	Routine. No 17129 Pte BOSWELL arrives from leave.	
		PM	Routine. visit & inspect 121 Fld Coy RE	

Army Form C. 2118.

WAR DIARY
or
INTELLIGENCE SUMMARY.
(Erase heading not required.)

Place	Date	Hour	Summary of Events and Information	Remarks and references to Appendices
ETRICOURT	1/11/17	AM	Routine. Visit Ytrés. 119 Heavy Batt. 14 R.S.Pk. 2/3 AHT, 121 RE. Div Hdqrs 16 RIR(?)	
		PM	Routine, Visit Ytrés 42 Labour Coy. MMD AC Cable Sec. RE. Attend Conference on D.R.S. officer	
	2/11/17	AM	Routine, Move PM in here MMD Vet Ytrés 121 RE & 7 RIR.	
		PM	Routine attend DADVS office during his absence.	
	3/11/17	AM	Routine attend DADVS office June in Vety Charge 51 R.F.A. "6" Pontoon Park	
		PM	Routine ADVS, III. IV, V Corps inspect section	
	4/11/17	AM	Routine Visit Ytrés, all units under Vety Charge. Church Parade for all ranks.	
		PM	Routine receive letter of congratulation from DVS on the section	
	5/11/17	AM	Routine Visit units under Vety Charge	
		PM	Routine Bath for men	
	6/11/17	AM	Routine evacuated 13 Mules 1 Mule to 7 Vety Hospital	
		PM	Routine Visit 7 RIR.	
	7/11/17	AM	Routine Juniors in Vety Charge 6 CRT, 700 Labour Coy, 48 Labour Coy	
		PM	Routine Juniors Vety Charge 408, 401, 409 Field Coy RE & 1/8 Royal Scots.	
	8/11/17	AM	Routine Visit inspected all units	
		PM	Routine attend conference at ADVS office	

Army Form C. 2118.

WAR DIARY
or
INTELLIGENCE SUMMARY.
(Erase heading not required.)

Instructions regarding War Diaries and Intelligence Summaries are contained in F. S. Regs., Part II, and the Staff Manual respectively. Title pages will be prepared in manuscript.

Place	Date	Hour	Summary of Events and Information	Remarks and references to Appendices
ETRICOURT	9/1/17	AM	Routine	
	9/1/17	PM	Routine	
	10/1/17	AM	Routine. Took over Vety Charge 51 Brd Arty Hors	
	10/1/17	PM	Routine. Had stampede horses	
	11/1/17	AM	Routine. Kaskes had action	
	11/1/17	PM	Routine	
	12/1/17	AM	Routine. Visit all unit under Vety Charge	
	12/1/17	PM	Routine. Visit 6 CRT.	
	13/1/17	AM	Routine. March 27 animals to No 7 VETY. HOSPITAL.	
	13/1/17	PM	Routine.	
	14/1/17	AM	Routine. Visit units under Vety Charge	
	14/1/17	PM	Routine. ADVS IV CORPS made return. Took on Charge IV CORPS, HORSE UNIT	
	15/1/17	AM	Routine. Visit surgical units under Vety Charge	
	15/1/17	PM	Routine. Attend Conference BTVO Office	
	16/1/17	AM	Routine. Visit surgical 40D 401, 404 Field Coy RE 51 Inf Depot to 15 Feb. b/o 7/17	
	16/1/17	PM	Routine. Attend DADVS office during his absence	G Mason

WAR DIARY
or
INTELLIGENCE SUMMARY.
(Erase heading not required.)

Army Form C. 2118.

Place	Date	Hour	Summary of Events and Information	Remarks and references to Appendices
ETRICOURT	17/4/17	AM	Routine Vet work under Vety Officer	
		PM	Routine. 51st Mobile Section going up need 48 MVS	
	18/4/17	AM	Routine. Elect Advanced Vety. Aid Post incl D.A.D.V.S. 36 Div	
		PM	Routine Forward report on SPECIFIC OPTHALMIA in DADVS"	
	19/4/17	AM	Routine. Went & arrange for A.V.A.P.	
		PM	Routine	
	20/4/17	AM	Routine Vet amb	
		PM	Routine. Examined 27 horses. Ordered to 7 Vety Hospital	
	21/4/17	AM	Routine Vet bidens. Posl. 12 CV M VS gas cases	
		PM	Routine Vet AVAP inspected and evacuated sick	
	22/4/17	AM	Routine 51st Div Mobile Section Sun Safine to Corps Cd	
		PM	Routine Evacuated 72 animals to no 7 VETY HOSPITAL	
	23/4/17	AM	Routine ADVS IV 3rd CAVALRY corps' Ind Sector	
		PM	Routine. Examined 78 animals to 5 Vety HOSPITAL	
	24/4/17	AM	Routine DVS. BCIS DDVS 3 Army Ind sector	
			Routine Also Evacuated valuable Vet amb	
		PM	Routine ADVS 14 "CORPS" Insp Sector	

WAR DIARY or INTELLIGENCE SUMMARY

Army Form C. 2118.

Place	Date	Hour	Summary of Events and Information	Remarks and references to Appendices
BROUAY	25/11/17	AM	Rubru 51st Div. MDS buses actor floor places 6 MAS GROS DIV	
		PM	Rubru 123 animal wounded to IVERY HOSPITAL	
	26/11/17	AM	Rubru evacuate 77 animals to 7 VET'Y HOSPITAL	
		PM	Rubru	
	27/11/17	AM	Rubru nalan and	
		PM	Rubru goun so much to ham for 6 CKT	
	28/11/17	AM	Rubru hand over MDS TCCS to 2nd RW MDS	
		PM	Rubru	
	29/11/17	AM	Coin van ERICOURT Church to ACHIET LE PETIT	
		PM		
	25/11/17	AM	leave ACHIET LEPETIT & arrive at FOSSEUX	
		PM	leave FOSSEUX arrive to ACHIET LE PETIT	

WAR DIARY
INTELLIGENCE SUMMARY.
(Erase heading not required.)

Army Form C. 2118.

Instructions regarding War Diaries and Intelligence Summaries are contained in F. S. Regs., Part II. and the Staff Manual respectively. Title pages will be prepared in manuscript.

Place	Date	Hour	Summary of Events and Information	Remarks and references to Appendices
Achiet-le-Petit	1/12/17	PM	March ACHIET LE PETIT	
POST.	1/12/17	PM	Arrive at BEAULENCOURT.	
Beaulencourt	2/12/17	AM	Leave BEAULENCOURT.	
	2/12/17	PM	Arrive ETRICOURT Y2 Central	
Etricourt	3/12/17	AM	Routine. Horse sick De SPAM'S 2 Division in evacuating horses	
	3/12/17	PM	Routine. DAD'S work extra	
	4/12/17	AM	Routine. Vet work	
	4/12/17	PM	Routine.	
	5/12/17	AM	Routine. Evacuate horses at YPRES Railhead	
	5/12/17	PM	Routine. Entrain horses at YPRES Railhead	
	6/12/17	AM	Routine. DOVS 2 Army v Brown detach next section	
	6/12/17	PM	Routine. Entrain horses at YPRES railhead	
	7/12/17	AM	Routine. Vet work under adj charge	
	7/12/17	PM	Routine. Entrain at YPRES railhead	
	8/12/17	AM	Routine. DAD'S work extra	
	8/12/17	PM	Routine. Entrain at Railhead	
			Routine. Rayhen	

Army Form C. 2118.

WAR DIARY
or
INTELLIGENCE SUMMARY.

(Erase heading not required.)

Instructions regarding War Diaries and Intelligence Summaries are contained in F. S. Regs., Part II. and the Staff Manual respectively. Title pages will be prepared in manuscript.

Place	Date	Hour	Summary of Events and Information	Remarks and references to Appendices
ETRICOURT	9/12/17	AM	Routine entrain at railhead	
		PM	Routine	
	10/12/17	AM	Routine Vet unit under vety. charge	
		PM	Routine entrain at railhead	
	11/12/17	AM	Routine DDVS VCIRS inspection	Both for men
		PM	Routine Vet unit under vety. charge	
	12/12/17	AM	Routine ADVS VCIRS Vet. Section	
		PM	Routine entrain at Railhead	
	13/12/17	AM	Routine DDVS 2nd Army Y insp. return	
		PM	Routine entrain at Railhead	
	14/12/17	AM	Routine Visit by ADVS	
		PM	Routine Landrover unit under vety. charge of Capt. M.R.C.V.S	
	15/12/17	AM	Routine DDVS 6 CORPS Vet. Section	
		PM	Routine entrain at Railhead	
	16/12/17	AM	Routine Dn unit under vety. charge	
		PM	Routine	

WAR DIARY
or
INTELLIGENCE SUMMARY.
(Erase heading not required.)

Army Form C. 2118.

Place	Date	Hour	Summary of Events and Information	Remarks and references to Appendices
ERVIDOURT	17/12/17		Move to COURCELLES LE COMPTE in snowstorm	
COURCELLES	18/12/17		Move to farm J.M SIGRENS between LABELLE V & T HUMBERCOURT	
LE COMPTE	19/12/17			
HUMBERCOURT	20/12/17		Move to HUMBERCOURT. Road in bad condition to due to thaw	
		AM	Routine, no rain, weather fine to fair for ten days	
		PM	Routine. Visit all sent in pledge	
	21/12/17	AM	Routine	
		PM	"	
	22/12/17	AM	Routine	
		PM	Move scelin to MONDICOURT.	
MONDICOURT	23/12/17	AM		
		PM	Routine. Viril ningled 222 FIELD Coy RE.	
	24/12/17	AM	DADVS evacuated to hospital has in ambu 7300V	
		PM		

WAR DIARY
or
INTELLIGENCE SUMMARY.

(Erase heading not required.)

Army Form C. 2118.

Place	Date	Hour	Summary of Events and Information	Remarks and references to Appendices
MONDICOURT	26/9/17	8 am	Routine. Visit Div Hqrs. See DADVS of 3rd Canadian. Stationery	
		1 pm		
	27/9/17	8 am	Routine	
		1 pm		
PUCHEVILLERS	27/9/17	8 am	Move to PUCHEVILLERS incl 168 BDE	
		1 pm		
CORBIE	28/9/17	8 am	Move to "CORBIE" area	
		1 pm		
	29/9/17	8 am	Routine. See DDVS 5th Army, stranded Section	
		1 pm		
	30/9/17	8 am	Routine. Visit stranded 121 Field Co RE 2026 RSC Div Hqrs Rear P.	
		1 pm		
	31/9/17	8 am	Routine. Visit stranded 107 Bde & 110 Field Ambulance	
		1 pm	Routine. S/I Allotson proceeds on leave.	

WAR DIARY
or
INTELLIGENCE SUMMARY.

Army Form C. 2118.

48 Mob Vet Sec

Place	Date	Hour	Summary of Events and Information	Remarks and references to Appendices
CORBIE	1/1/18	AM	Routine. Vet inspect 107 Bde horse lines XIX Corps	
		PM	Routine. Vet off. went sick. MDS	
	2/1/18	AM	Routine. Chas. from Red Cross XIII Corps	
		PM	Routine. Vet transport No 2 C. sub. Maun	
	3/1/18	AM	Routine. Inspt. wells with R.V.O. 107 Bde	
		PM	Routine. Vet inspd. wing wels. Reg. Charge	
	4/1/18	AM	Routine. BMVS Thurs. Stores and Subs.	
		PM	Routine. Inspd. wels with BMVS XIII Corps	
	5/1/18	AM	Routine. evacuate 16 animals to 14 Vety Hospital	
		PM	Routine. Rfse inspd arms	
	6/1/18	AM	Routine. Vet takes KIT.	
		PM	Routine.	
	7/1/18	AM	Self. Car CORBIE taun at MARBONNIERE	
		PM	Routine.	
	8/1/18	AM	Routine. Inspect animals of 5th Army Sup horse Coys.	
		PM	Routine.	

Army Form C. 2118.

WAR DIARY
or
INTELLIGENCE SUMMARY.
(Erase heading not required.)

Place	Date	Hour	Summary of Events and Information	Remarks and references to Appendices
HARBONNIERES	9/1/18	AM	Routine. Inspect and meet Vety Charge	
		PM	Routine	
"	10/1/18	AM	Routine. Inspect Sty A.S.C	
		PM	Routine. Saw answers	
"	11/1/18	AM	Routine	
		PM	Routine	
	12/1/18	AM	Evacuate 12 animals to No 7 VETY. Hospital. Orders move to	
NESLE		PM	NESLE	
"	13/1/18	AM	Routine. Inspect SW Ly Cy. Send draspels from 7 4 hers to 107	
		PM	Routine. Drew food from Field Cashier 18 Co KiOS	
"	14/1/18	AM	Leave NESLE and arrive at	
AUBIGNY		PM	AUBIGNY	
"	15/1/18	AM	Visit DOUCHY. FLEQUIERS BOUVY and D.A.D.V.S	
		PM	Visit French Hospital at ESTOUILLY and report on available Stb to DDVS for PM	
"	16/1/18	AM	Inspect AUBIGNY and Major DVRY replies dispatch orders to move to ST. SIMON	
		PM	Routine	

[Stamp: OFFICER COMMANDING 42TH MOBILE VETERINARY SECTION A.V.C. Date 31.1.18]

J. Moore
Captain

WAR DIARY
or
INTELLIGENCE SUMMARY.
(Erase heading not required.)

Army Form C. 2118.

Place	Date	Hour	Summary of Events and Information	Remarks and references to Appendices
17/1/18 ST. SIMON	17/1/18	Am	Move to St. Simon	
		Pm	Routine	
	18/1/18	Am	Routine. Stamped the village of St. Simon	
		Pm	Routine. Road stamped 2LM G. Cy.	
	19/1/18	Am	Routine. Unit engaged all but 2 of Cy.C.	
		Pm	Routine. ESDVS Road routine	
	20/1/18	Am	Routine. Stamped village of FAUCOURT. evacuate 22 animal to 7 VH	
		Pm	Routine. Stamped village of BROCUT.	
	21/1/18	Am	Routine. Stamped villages of GRAND SERAUCOURT.	
		Pm	Routine. "	
	22/1/18	Am	Routine. Unit engaged all week	
		Pm	Routine	
	23/1/18	Am	Routine. Stamped village of BENY. ST. CHRISTOPHE	
		Pm	Routine	
	24/1/18	Am	Routine. Stamped village of OLLEZY.	
		Pm	Routine. Attend anxience stores afair	

Officer Commanding
48th Mobile Veterinary Section A.V.C.
Date 31.1.18

Army Form C. 2118.

WAR DIARY
or
INTELLIGENCE SUMMARY.
(Erase heading not required.)

Instructions regarding War Diaries and Intelligence Summaries are contained in F. S. Regs., Part II. and the Staff Manual respectively. Title pages will be prepared in manuscript.

Place	Date	Hour	Summary of Events and Information	Remarks and references to Appendices
ST. SIMON	25/1/18	AM	Rechie Evacuated 20 animals to No 7 Vet Hospital	
		PM	Rechie about inspecting stores Affine	
	26/1/18	AM	Rechie Read all work under V/Charge	
		PM	Rechie Evacuated village of OLLEZY.	
	27/1/18	AM	Rechie Vist Cmys TRAIN	
		PM	Rechie Vail unit	
	29/1/18	AM	Rechie Evacuated Pony at BUSIGNY	
		PM	Rechie had all unit	
	29/1/18	AM	Rechie KSRA was seeten	
		PM	Rechie Vist Cys TRAIN	
	30/1/18	AM	Rechie Evacuated Vlegs DAK m P S	
		PM	Rechie Vist Horse	
	31/1/18	AM	Rechie KSRA vet seen Inspected Animal for evacuation	
	1/1/18	PM	Rechie Attend Inquira 5000 force	

Alfred Odam

Diary from 78 Mob Vet Secⁿ

WAR DIARY
or
INTELLIGENCE SUMMARY

Army Form C. 2118

D.A.D.V.S.
36TH (ULSTER) DIVISION
No. V.S. 1024
Date 28.2.18

Place	Date	Hour	Summary of Events and Information	Remarks and references to Appendices
ST. SIMON.	1/2/18	AM	Routine - Evacuated 444 animals to 7 VETY. HOSPITAL. Disinfected standings at AUBIGNY.	
.	.	PM	Routine.	
do.	2/2/18	AM	Routine. Disinfect standings at ARTEMPS. attnd board of Furriers at No. 3 Coy Div TRAIN	
		PM	Routine. DADVS 36 Division visits section.	
do	3/2/18	AM	Routine. Disinfect standings at HAPPENCOURT. mallein 53 horses of 36 M.G. Co. at G^d SERAUCOURT.	
		PM	Routine. Disinfect standings at BROUCHY.	
do	4/2/18	AM	Routine. Disinfect standings at TUGNY	
		PM	Routine. Disinfecting party at TUGNY. Evacuate 25 animals to No. 7 VET H.O.S.	
do	5/2/18	AM	Routine.	
		PM	Routine.	
do	6/2/18	AM	Routine. Disinfecting party at DURY.	
		PM	Routine. Draw 1000 francs from FIELD CASHIER. STAFF SGT JAMES. SGT BARRATT present	
do	7/2/18	AM	Routine. disinfecting party at TUGNY. On 14 sick cases Paid men	

J. Smith Captⁿ
A.V.C.

WAR DIARY
or
INTELLIGENCE SUMMARY.

Army Form C. 2118.

Place	Date	Hour	Summary of Events and Information	Remarks and references to Appendices
ST SIMON	8/12	AM	Routine. Disinfecting party at CUGNY.	
		PM	Routine.	
	9/12	AM	Routine. Disinfecting party at CUGNY.	
		PM	Routine.	
	10/12	AM	Routine. Disinfecting party at CUGNY.	
		PM	Routine. Disinfecting party at DURY.	
	11/12	AM	Routine. Disinfecting party at AUBIGNY (St)	
		PM	Routine. Disinfecting party at OLLEZY	
	12/12	AM	Routine. Disinfecting party at VILLESELVE arrived 21 arrived to YVET HOS.	
		PM	Routine. Disinfecting party at AUBIGNY. Baths for men.	
	13/12	AM	Routine. Disinfecting party at VILLESELVE. CAPT CHOWN proceed on	
		PM	leave Capt GUERTIN assumes duties of OC H8 M.I.S. Rifle inspection	
	14/12	AM	Routine. Disinfecting party at PITHON.	
		PM	Routine. Disinfecting party at ESTOUILLY.	
	15/12	AM	Routine. Disinfecting party at VILLESELVE.	
		PM	Routine. Pay men.	

WAR DIARY
or
INTELLIGENCE SUMMARY.

Army Form C. 2118.

Place	Date	Hour	Summary of Events and Information	Remarks and references to Appendices
ST SIMON	16/9/18	A.M	Routine. DISINFECTING PARTY AT LE HAMEL	
		P.M	Routine	
	17/9/18	A.M	Routine. DISINFECTING PARTY AT VILLESELVE	
		P.M	Routine. Church parade for men	
	18/9/18	A.M	Routine. Rifle inspection	
		P.M	Routine	
	19/9/18	A.M	Routine. 2 animals to 7 VETY HOSPITAL	
		P.M	Routine. Baths for men. Gas Bootgrease for archives.	
	20/9/18	A.M	Routine. Visit & inspect 179 Bde RFA	
		P.M	Routine	
	21/9/18	A.M	Routine. Disinfecting party at BRAY ST CHRISTOPHE	
		P.M	Routine. F.O.V.S. XVIII Corps visit to show Bay men	
	22/9/18	A.M	Routine. Disinfecting party at ANNOIS	
		P.M	Routine. Evacuate 26 animal to 7 VET HOSPITAL	
	23/9/18	A.M	Routine. Limber & waggon cleaning	
		P.M	Routine. Rifle Inspection	

Army Form C. 2118.

WAR DIARY
or
INTELLIGENCE SUMMARY.
(Erase heading not required.)

Place	Date	Hour	Summary of Events and Information	Remarks and references to Appendices
St Simon	24/2/18	A.M	Routine	
		P.M	Routine Sgt Schofield proceeded on 14 Days leave.	
	25/2/18	A.M	Routine S/Sgt James, Sergt Barrett. Returned off leave.	
		P.M	Routine	
	26/2/18	A.M	Routine Evacuate 2 q Animals to No 4 Vety Hospital.	
		P.M	Routine	
	27/2/18	A.M	Routine D.A.D.V.S. Visited Lines.	
		P.M	Routine	
	28/2/18	A.M	Routine	
		P.M	Routine	

Army Form C. 2118.

WAR DIARY
or
INTELLIGENCE SUMMARY.
(Erase heading not required.)

48TH MOBILE VETERINARY SECTION.

Place	Date	Hour	Summary of Events and Information	Remarks and references to Appendices
Field	1/2/15	A.M	Routine. Took over duties from Capt. Jo. Quertin.	
		P.M	Routine	
	2/3/15	A.M	Routine. Visit arrival Div' HQrs	
		P.M	Routine	
	3/2/15	am	Routine. Visit Bhq Ask Horse Ph & Lime	
		pm	Routine	
	4/2/15	am	Routine. Visit No 184 Coy ASC.	
		pm	Routine. ADVS XVIII Corps mob hospls ʃtcbn	
	5/2/15	am	Routine. Lud 30 animal to 7 mby hospital BDSW. Visit mules	
		pm	Routine. Visit 2q ASC	
	6/3/15	am	Routine. Vet at work mules ucg change	
		pm	Routine. DBSW visit ʃtcbn	
	7/2/15	am	Routine. Vet at work mules UCG change	
		pm	Routine. ADVS XVIII Corps visit ringworm Stcbn	
	8/2/15	am	Routine. Sul 11 animals to 7VTH Hospital. Inspect 26y ASC records	
		pm	Routine. Inspect remounts 9 DIV Iron hill DTOUS	

Major OUR

Army Form C. 2118.

WAR DIARY
or
INTELLIGENCE SUMMARY.
(Erase heading not required.)

Instructions regarding War Diaries and Intelligence Summaries are contained in F. S. Regs., Part II. and the Staff Manual respectively. Title pages will be prepared in manuscript.

Place	Date	Hour	Summary of Events and Information	Remarks and references to Appendices
ST SIMON	9/3/18	AM	Routine. Made P.M. in lieu 3 day O.S.C. (Hospital lis)	
		PM	Routine. Attend 20" Div' STEEPLE CHASES at ERCHEU.	
	10/3/18	AM	Routine. Inspect train detachment at SUZY	
		PM	Routine. Visit units and M.D.Rs.	
	11/3/18	AM	Routine. Saw O.C. 23 Divements at 10A.M. Schedule seen to work	
		PM	Routine. Commence new J. Lecture on sick management at ARTEMPS	
	12/3/18	AM	Routine. Evacuate 53 sick animals from H.A.M. to No 7 VET'Y. HOSPITAL	
		PM	Routine. Visit all CO's train Lecture at ARTEMPS	
	13/3/18	PM	Routine. Lecture inspected at ST SIMON by Br' General Y CORPS.	
		PM	Routine. Lecture at ARTEMPS	
	14/3/18	AM	Routine. Visit units sw' H94.	
		PM	Routine. Attend Engineer horses from Lecture at ARTEMPS.	
	15/3/18	AM	Routine. 21 animals transferred to No 7 VET'Y. HOSPITAL	
		PM	Routine. Lecture at ARTEMPS.	
	16/3/18	AM	Routine. O.A.T.P. 26 Division visits within	
		PM	Routine. Rain new.	

OFFICER COMMANDING
No........
Date 31/3/18
MOBILE VETERINARY SECTION A.V.C.

[signature] Capt

Army Form C. 2118.

WAR DIARY
or
INTELLIGENCE SUMMARY.
(Erase heading not required.)

Instructions regarding War Diaries and Intelligence Summaries are contained in F.S. Regs., Part II. and the Staff Manual respectively. Title pages will be prepared in manuscript.

Place	Date	Hour	Summary of Events and Information	Remarks and references to Appendices
ST SIMON	17/3/18	AM	Routine. Attend. 61st DIV. HORSE SHOW. Spyke Jumping & Officer Chger	
		PM	Routine. Vet no 3 by age.	
	18/3/18	AM	Routine. Assume duties of O.C.M.V.S. 36 DIV vice MAJOR HORNER on leave	
		PM	Routine. Vet all ops train. Lecture at BRETEMPS	
	19/3/18	AM	Routine. Evacuate 23 animals to 1 VET HOSPITAL from Lyn	
		PM	Routine. Lecture at BRETEMPS	
	20/3/18	AM	Routine. Visit Remount section ABBEVILLE	
		PM	Routine.	
	21/3/18	AM	Routine. Lecture.	
		PM	Routine. H.Q.M.V.S. moved to BROCOMP. Inwards movements of evacuation to Corps	
	22/3/18	AM	Routine. section move to enemy retire.	
		PM	Lectine moves to LIGNEREMONT.	
	23/3/18	AM	Section moves to BEAULIEU. Fired all 10 s.	
		PM	— Casualty return to DDVS XVIII Corps. —	
	24/3/18	AM	Section moves from Beaulieu to ???	
		PM	—	Wham Capt.

[Stamp: OFFICER COMMANDING MOBILE VETERINARY SECTION A.V.C. No. ... Date 21/3/18]

Army Form C. 2118.

WAR DIARY
or
INTELLIGENCE SUMMARY.
(Erase heading not required.)

Instructions regarding War Diaries and Intelligence Summaries are contained in F. S. Regs., Part II. and the Staff Manual respectively. Title pages will be prepared in manuscript.

Place	Date	Hour	Summary of Events and Information	Remarks and references to Appendices
Field	25/3/18	AM	Section move from AVRICOURT to GERBEAUCOURT.	
		PM		
	26/3/18	AM	Section move from GERBEAUCOURT to COULLEMELLE	
		PM		
	27/3/18	AM	Section move from COULLEMELLE to LOUVRECHY.	
		PM		
	28/3/18	AM	Section move from LOUVRECHY to LAWARDE	
		PM		
	29/3/18	AM	Section move from LAWARDE to TAISNIL	
		PM		
	30/3/18	AM	Section moves from TAISNIL to ALLERY.	
		PM		
	31/3/18	AM	Section moves from Allery to Beauchamps.	
		PM		

WAR DIARY
INTELLIGENCE SUMMARY

Army Form C. 2118.

(Erase heading not required.)

Place	Date	Hour	Summary of Events and Information	Remarks and references to Appendices
BEAUCHAMPS	1/4/18	PM	Vet Div¹ Hqrs inspected Hqr Chargers	Formation of 4.M.V.S. 20-8-15.
do	2/4/18	PM	Routine under orders to move to NORTH.	Date proceeding overseas from UK 3-10-15
do	3/4/18	AM	Routine.	9 N.L. 31
		PM		
Zutkerque	4/4/18	AM	Section arrived at FEUQUIERES.	
		PM		
	5/4/18	AM	Section arrived at PROVEN.	
		PM	Routine	
	6/4/18	AM	Routine visit outpost 36 DIV TRAIN less No 1 Coy	
		P.M.	Routine B.A.V.S. returns from leave stayed at chateau	
	7/4/18	AM	Routine. Vet 1st Fat. M.V.S. training to keep in standing	
		PM	Routine inspected Fort Rihin DIK move to ELVERDINGE.	
ELVERDINGE	8/4/18	AM	ASVS, II Corps vets section	
		PM	DADVS Visited Section	

Army Form C. 2118.

WAR DIARY
or
INTELLIGENCE SUMMARY.
(Erase heading not required.)

Instructions regarding War Diaries and Intelligence Summaries are contained in F.S. Regs., Part II. and the Staff Manual respectively. Title pages will be prepared in manuscript.

Place	Date	Hour	Summary of Events and Information	Remarks and references to Appendices
ELVERDINGHE	9/4/15	am	Routine. deport 6 animals to 6" CORPS evacuation station.	Formation of #4 M.V.S. 20.3.15. Date-proceeding overseas from UK
		pm	Routine	
	10/4/15	am	Routine. horses walk exercise. harness & kit.	
		pm	Routine. road all men b.train.	
	11/4/15	am	Routine. 6 animals to C.E.S.	Ranks & for horse
		pm	Routine	
	12/4/15	am	Routine. road all work 1st TRAIN	
		pm	Routine	
	13/4/15	am	Routine. inspect stables	
		pm	Routine	DIC
	14/4/15	am	Routine. attend conference DDVS Ypres	
		pm	Routine	
	15/4/15	am	Routine. KBSTS med. section	
		pm	Routine. evacuate 7 cases to VES	
	16/4/15	am	Routine. hors. section to PROVEN and c/K very badly shelled	
		pm	Routine	

T2134. Wt. W708—776. 500000. 4/15. Sir J.C. & S.

Army Form C. 2118.

WAR DIARY
or
INTELLIGENCE SUMMARY.
(Erase heading not required.)

Instructions regarding War Diaries and Intelligence Summaries are contained in F. S. Regs., Part II. and the Staff Manual respectively. Title pages will be prepared in manuscript.

Place	Date	Hour	Summary of Events and Information	Remarks and references to Appendices
PROVEN.	17/4/18	pm	Routine. Arrange for evacuation of sick at 2 Corps. V.E.S.	
		pm	Routine.	
	18/4/18	am	Routine. Attend Conference 9am.	
		pm	Routine. Inspected Divl. Sig. Co. R.E. 55th Div. HQR. horses.	
	19/4/18	am	Routine. Evacuation 6 cases to 2 Corps V.S.	
		pm	Routine. All well with team.	
	20/4/18	am	Routine. ADVS visit section.	
		pm	Routine.	
	21/4/18	am	Routine. Inspected all mules 5th TRAIN.	
		pm	Routine. Visit 2nd Echn. R. & E.C.	
	22/4/18	am	Routine. ADVS 6 Corps visit section.	
		pm	Routine. All well.	
	23/4/18	am	Routine. Visit 9th FD. SIG Co. R.E.	
		pm	Routine.	
	24/4/18	am	Routine. Inspected all mules 5th TRAIN.	
		pm	Routine.	

Maurice Capps

Army Form C. 2118.

WAR DIARY
or
INTELLIGENCE SUMMARY.
(Erase heading not required.)

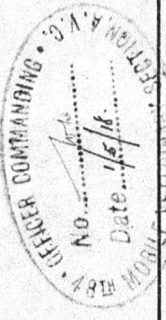

Place	Date	Hour	Summary of Events and Information	Remarks and references to Appendices
EVERDINGHE	25/4/16	12n	Routine work work	
		Pm	Routine attend conference SDSVS offs	
	26/4/16	8m	Routine Jam re to rifle range & pass hrs & Rustwy	
		Pm	Routine work vet work	
	27/4/16	8m	Routine march 30 animals to VES	
		Pm	Routine SDSVS inspect MVS & all oys. ext. TRAIN	
	28/4/16	8m	Routine glanders 24 FRENCH ARMY hors to 2 CORPS. VES	
		Pm	Routine work all vet wor	
	29/4/16	8m	Routine march	
		Pm	Routine —	
	30/4/16	8m	Routine SDSVS work action	
		Pm	Routine	

Moor GH

WAR DIARY
or
INTELLIGENCE SUMMARY.

Army Form C. 2118.

Place	Date	Hour	Summary of Events and Information	Remarks and references to Appendices
Elverdinghe	1/5/16	AM	Routine	
		PM	Routine	
PROVEN	2/5/16	AM	Routine. Evacuated 6 animals to V.E.S	
		PM	Routine. Inspect kennel of 36 Div TRAIN.	
"	3/5/16	AM	Routine. Evacuated 17 animals to V.E.S	
		PM	Routine. Evacuated 31 animals to V.E.S	
"	4/5/16	AM	Routine. Evacuated 23 animals to V.E.S	
		PM	Routine. Draw 1500 Francs from FIELD CASHIER - Paid men.	
"	5/5/16	AM	Routine. Evacuated 8 animals to V.E.S.	
		PM	Routine. Visit D.H.Q. R.E	
"	6/5/16	AM	Routine. Evacuated 13 animals to V.E.S.	
		PM	Routine. Visit & inspect 36 DIV. SIG. Co.	
"	7/5/16	AM	Routine. Visit & inspect H.Qr units	
		PM	Routine.	

Army Form C. 2118.

WAR DIARY
or
INTELLIGENCE SUMMARY.
(Erase heading not required.)

Instructions regarding War Diaries and Intelligence Summaries are contained in F. S. Regs., Part II. and the Staff Manual respectively. Title pages will be prepared in manuscript.

Place	Date	Hour	Summary of Events and Information	Remarks and references to Appendices
ROUEN	8/5/18	AM	Routine. Evacuate 17 animals to V.E.S.	
		PM	Routine. Horse from C/331 Bde. dies.	
	9/5/18	AM	Routine. Evacuate 13 animals to V.E.S.	
		PM	Routine. — A.D.V.S. II Corps visits & inspects section	
	10/5/18	AM	Routine. paid men	
		PM	Routine. H.B. horse dies. PM Rupture of LARGE COLON	Appx
	11/5/18	AM	Routine. D.A.D.S.S. 36 Div. visits section.	
		PM	Routine. 12 animals evacuated to V.E.S.	
	12/5/18	AM	Routine. 9 animals evacuated to V.E.S.	
		PM	Routine. Visit 7 suspect units under sky charge.	
	13/5/18	AM	Routine. 11 animals evacuated to V.E.S. visit D.H.Q. Div Sig. C.	
		PM	Routine.	
	14/5/18	AM	Routine. A.D.V.S. 36 Div. inspects MOBILIZATION STORES of 48 M.V.S.	
		PM	Routine.	
	15/5/18	AM	Routine. Evacuate 16 animals to V.E.S.	
		PM	Routine.	

Army Form C. 2118.

WAR DIARY
or
INTELLIGENCE SUMMARY.
(Erase heading not required.)

Instructions regarding War Diaries and Intelligence Summaries are contained in F. S. Regs., Part II. and the Staff Manual respectively. Title pages will be prepared in manuscript.

Place	Date	Hour	Summary of Events and Information	Remarks and references to Appendices
PROVEN.	16/12	AM	Routine.	
		PM	Routine. 12 animals evacuated to V.E.S.	
	17/12	AM	Routine.	
		PM	Routine. (OPEN) MAJOR GENERAL inspects section	
	18/12	AM	Routine. 11 animals evacuated to Vet. S.	
		PM	Routine.	
	19/12	AM	Routine. Inspection of Saddlery. Rifles. Bandoliers.	
		PM	Routine. Rifle drill.	
	20/12	AM	Routine. DADVS 36 Div vets section. Evacuate 11 animals to V.E.S.	
		PM	Routine.	
	21/12	AM	Routine. Visit & inspect. 36. DIV. TRAIN. horses	
		PM	Routine.	
	22/12	AM	Routine. Evacuate 11 animals to V.E.S.	
		PM	Routine. Visit DADVS 2 ARMY. with RADVS 36 DIVN Drew 500 fr from FIELD CASHIER	
	23/12	AM	Routine. Evacuate 11 animals to V.E.S. DADVS 36 Div vets section	
		PM	Routine. attend conference DADVS 36 Div office	

Army Form C. 2118.

WAR DIARY
or
INTELLIGENCE SUMMARY.
(Erase heading not required.)

Place	Date	Hour	Summary of Events and Information	Remarks and references to Appendices
PROVEN	24/10/18	AM	Routine visit 36 D.S.Co r36 Div Train.	
		PM	Routine pay men	
	25/10/18	AM	Routine evacuate 6 animals to V.E.S	
		PM	Routine visit 36 D.H.QRS	
	26/10/18	AM	Routine	
		PM	Routine	
	27/10/18	AM	Routine. 7 animals evacuated to V.E.S.	
		PM	Routine	
	28/10/18	AM	Routine Evac 8 animals to V.E.S.	
		PM	Routine	
	29/10/18	AM	Routine Evac 6 animals to V.E.S.	
		PM	Routine	
	30/10/18	AM	Routine D.A.D.V.S 36 Div visits section	
		PM	Routine Attend conference at DADVS 36 Div	
	31/10/18	AM	Routine.	
		PM	Routine visit all units under vety charge.	

WAR DIARY or INTELLIGENCE SUMMARY

Army Form C. 2118.

27. 48th Mob. Vet. Sect.

Formed 30-8-15

Annual returns 5-10-15

Vol 33

Place	Date	Hour	Summary of Events and Information	Remarks and references to Appendices
RVYEN	1/7/18	AM	Routine. Evacuate 7 animals to V.E.S.	
		PM	Routine. attended Board of Shoeing at No 1 Co. A.S.C. 36 DIV.TRN.	
	2/7/18	AM	Routine. inspection of VETY EQUIPMENT	
		PM	Routine.	
	3/7/18	AM	Routine. Evacuate 11 animals to V.E.S.	
		PM	Routine. visit & inspect 36 DIV SIG Coy RE. 100 francs FM CASHIER	
	4/7/18	AM	Routine. Shoesmithy. - Box Reprals inspection	
		PM	Routine. Paid men.	
	5/7/18	AM	Routine. Evacuate 10. animals.	
		PM	Routine. visit & inspect. 840.RE. RA. MMP.	
	6/7/18	AM	Routine. Evacuate 6 animals to V.E.S	
		PM	Routine. admit 5 MANGE from VAUX H.T. attend conference.	
	7/7/18	AM	Routine	
		PM	Routine. visit & inspect VETY EQUIPMENT.	
	8/7/18	AM	Routine inspect VETY EQUIPMENT.	
		PM	Routine. attended & animals for casting.	

Army Form C. 2118.

D.A.D.V.S.
36TH
(ULSTER) DIVISION.

No. ....
Date ....

WAR DIARY
or
INTELLIGENCE SUMMARY.
(Erase heading not required.)

Instructions regarding War Diaries and Intelligence Summaries are contained in F. S. Regs., Part II. and the Staff Manual respectively. Title pages will be prepared in manuscript.

Place	Date	Hour	Summary of Events and Information	Remarks and references to Appendices
ROUEN	9/6/18	AM	Routine evacuate Hannals to 2 ARMY F/D REM. SEC.	
		PM	Routine CPL LONSDALE returns from ANTI.GAS. SCHOOL	
	10/6/18	AM	Routine Gas lecture.	
		PM	Routine.	
	11/6/18	AM	Routine Evacuate of animals to V.E.S.	
		PM	Routine. Sinclairs inspection find men	
	12/6/18	AM	Routine. Inspection Rifles Bandoliers	
		PM	Routine inspect mules under vety charge.	
	13/6/18	AM	Routine Evacuats of animals to V.E.S.	
		PM	Routine	
	14/6/18	AM	Routine Evacuate of animals to V.E.S.	
		PM	Routine	
	15/6/18	AM	Routine inspect 36 DIV TRN. DADVS visits section	
		PM	Routine inspect VETY EQUIPMENT.	
	16/6/18	AM	Routine Fire Drill	
		PM	Routine	

WAR DIARY
or
INTELLIGENCE SUMMARY.
(Erase heading not required.)

Army Form C. 2118.

Instructions regarding War Diaries and Intelligence Summaries are contained in F. S. Regs., Part II. and the Staff Manual respectively. Title pages will be prepared in manuscript.

Place	Date	Hour	Summary of Events and Information	Remarks and references to Appendices
PROVEN	17/6/18	AM	Routine. DDVS II Army, ADVS II Corps & DADVS 36 Div visit section	
do		PM	Routine. Evacuate 9 animals to V.E.S.	
do	18/6/18	AM	Routine. DADVS 36 Div visits section. Bath of men	
do		PM	Routine. ADVS II Corps & AMERICAN COLONEL inspect section	
do	19/6/18	AM	Routine. Evacuate 5 animals to V.E.S.	
do		PM	Routine. PAID men	
do	20/6/18	AM	Routine. Visit 36 Div S.G.Co.	
do		PM	Routine. Attend conference S.A.D.V.S. 36 Div officer	
do	21/6/18	AM	Routine. Visit & inspect all units under Vety/charge.	
do		PM	Routine.	
do	22/6/18	AM	Routine. Evacuate 9 animals to V.E.S.	
do		PM	Routine. Visit No 1 & 2 Coy Div TRAIN	
do	23/6/18	AM	Routine. Rifle inspection	
do		PM	Routine. Visit DHQ & R.E., R.A. & MMP	
do	24/6/18	AM	Routine. Box Repair inspection	
do		PM	Routine.	

WAR DIARY or INTELLIGENCE SUMMARY.

Army Form C. 2118.

D.A.D.V.S., 36TH (ULSTER DIVISION)

Place	Date	Hour	Summary of Events and Information	Remarks and references to Appendices
PROVEN	25/6/18	AM	Routine. D.A.D.V.S 36 Div inspects AF 1098 Stores	
		PM	Routine. enemali 5 arrivals to V.E.S	
	26/6/18	AM	Routine	
		PM	Routine. visit 36 Div SIG.C.	
	27/6/18	AM	Routine. Interview with D.A.D.V.S 36 Div 17 Research	
		PM	Routine. I paid men chew 500/- from FLD CASHIER	
	28/6/18	AM	Routine. visit & inspect 36 Div TRAIN	
		PM	Routine. "	
	29/6/18	AM	Routine. enemali 4 arrivals to V.E.S	
		PM	Routine. inspect Vety equipment	
	30/6/18	AM	Routine. enemali 5 arrival to V.E.S.	
		PM	Routine	

48th Mobile Vety Section 36

Army Form C. 2118.

19

Section arrived
Overseas 5·10·15
Section formed 20.8.15

D.A.D.V.S.
36TH (ULSTER DIVISION).
No VD.1698
Date 1.8.18

WAR DIARY
or
INTELLIGENCE SUMMARY.
(Erase heading not required.)

Place	Date	Hour	Summary of Events and Information	Remarks and references to Appendices
PROVEN	1/4/18	AM	Routine attend 36 Div HORSE SHOW	
		PM	Routine	
do	2/4/18	AM	Routine tomortii arrivals to V.E.S.	
		PM	Routine	
LE SCHAEKE	3/4/18	AM	Section moves	
		PM		
do	4/4/18	AM	Routine	
		PM	Routine attend conference D.A.D.V.S. office	
do	5/4/18	AM	Routine. visit D.H.Q. M.M.P. Dn S/C Co.	
		PM	Routine. Rain new	
do	6/4/18	AM	Routine look up site for M.V.S.	
		PM	Routine	
	7/4/18	AM	Routine tomortii 2. animals to 10 V.E.S	
		PM	Routine. wrote to P34 D.I.2 Short 27.	
	8/4/18	AM	Routine visit + inspect 36 Dn TRAIN	
		PM	Routine	

Army Form C. 2118.

WAR DIARY
or
INTELLIGENCE SUMMARY.
(Erase heading not required.)

Instructions regarding War Diaries and Intelligence Summaries are contained in F. S. Regs., Part II. and the Staff Manual respectively. Title pages will be prepared in manuscript.

Place	Date	Hour	Summary of Events and Information	Remarks and references to Appendices
P.34.D.1.7	9/9/18	AM	DADVS visits section	
		PM	Routine	
	10/9/18	AM	Collect LD Horse of No 1 Sec DAC from FERME D HAEZE	
		PM	Routine visit and inspect. D.H.Q. 15 Coy. R.E. R.A. M.M.P.	
	11/9/18	AM	Routine Evacuate 4 animals to 10 V.E.S.	
		PM	Routine paid men.	
	12/9/18	AM	Routine Evacuate 8 animals to 10 V.E.S.	
		PM	Routine	
	13/9/18	AM	Routine visit & inspect 2 Coy ASC & 4 Coy ASC.	
		PM	Routine Fire drill.	
	14/9/18	AM	Routine Evacuate 9 animals to 10 V.E.S	
		PM	Routine Church Parade	
	15/9/18	AM	Routine Evacuate 13 animals to 10.V.E.S.	
		PM	Routine Baths for men.	
	16/9/18	AM	Routine	
		PM	Routine D.A.D.V.S visits & inspects horses of 30 Div TRAIN	

Army Form C. 2118.

WAR DIARY
or
INTELLIGENCE SUMMARY.
(Erase heading not required.)

Instructions regarding War Diaries and Intelligence Summaries are contained in F. S. Regs., Part II. and the Staff Manual respectively. Title pages will be prepared in manuscript.

Place	Date	Hour	Summary of Events and Information	Remarks and references to Appendices
Sheet 24 Pt d 12	14.4.16	AM	Routine. Evacuate 5 animals to 10 V.E.S.	
		PM	Routine	
	18.4.16	AM	Routine. Evacuate 13 animals to 10 V.E.S.	
		PM	Routine	
	19.4.16	AM	Routine. Paid run.	
		PM	Routine	
	20.4.16	AM	Routine. Evacuate 4 animals to 10 V.E.S.	
		PM	Routine	
	21.4.16	AM	Routine. Visit and inspect Div Sig Coy RE	
		PM	Routine. Visit and inspect MMP. RE. RA.	
	22.4.16	PM	Routine	
		PM	Routine. Visit & inspect No 1 & 3 Coy ASC	
	23.4.16	AM	Routine. Visit & inspect No 2 & 4 Coy TRN.	
		PM	Routine	
	24.4.16	AM	Routine. ADVS X CORPS visits section	
		PM	Routine	

Army Form C. 2118.

WAR DIARY
or
INTELLIGENCE SUMMARY.
(Erase heading not required.)

Instructions regarding War Diaries and Intelligence Summaries are contained in F. S. Regs., Part II. and the Staff Manual respectively. Title pages will be prepared in manuscript.

Place	Date	Hour	Summary of Events and Information	Remarks and references to Appendices
P3et D.I.2.	25/7/18	AM	Routine. 5 sick animals evacuated to 10 V.E.S	
		PM.	Routine. Attend conference.	
	26/7/18	AM	Routine. Visit & inspect 36 D. Sup. Co.	
		PM	Routine. Paid men.	
	27/7/18	AM	Routine. Visit inspect H.Q, 1 Coy & 2 Coy A.S.C	
		PM	Routine. Visit inspect 3 Coy & 4 Coy A.S.C.	
	28/7/18	AM	Routine. Visit inspect 69, 142, 188 L.A.B. Coys.	
		PM	Routine.	
	29/7/18	AM	Routine. 6 sick animals evacuated to 10 V.E.S	
		PM	Routine. 6 men invalids at 109. F.A.	
	30/7/18	AM	Routine. Visit & inspect 8 Can Rly Troops. 174 L.R.B. Co.	
		PM	Routine.	
	31/7/18	AM	Routine. 7 sick animals to 10 V.E.S	
		PM	Routine. 6 men invalided	

27

48 Foots Vety Sec. 36

WAR DIARY
or
INTELLIGENCE SUMMARY.
(Erase heading not required.)

Army Form C. 2118.

5-10-15 Arrived overseas
20.8. = 151 mobilised

D.A.D.V.S.
UNITED DIVISION.
No. V.D./8.3.M.
Date M881.9.8.

Place	Date	Hour	Summary of Events and Information	Remarks and references to Appendices
SHEET 27C				
P34.D1.2	1/8/18	AM	Routine. Visit - vinepick all unit under Vety Charge	
		PM	Routine. Attend Conference S.D.V.S. Office	
	2/8/18	AM	Routine. Evacuate 6 animals 16 X Corps V.F.S.	
		PM	Routine.	
	3/8/18	AM	Routine. Visit all units under Vety Charge	
		PM	Routine. Attend funeral at "ECKE"	
	4/8/18	AM	Routine. Attend Commemoration Service M'orning at TERDIGHEM	
		PM	Routine.	
	5/8/18	AM PM	Routine. Visit Horse Show EPERLEQUES	
	6/8/18	AM PM	Routine. Visit all units under Vety Charge	
	7/8/18	AM PM	Routine. Visit V.E.S. 10 Corps	
	8/8/18	AM	Routine. Visit all units here	
		PM	Routine. Attend conference S.D.V.S. Office	
	9/8/18	AM	Routine. Van on units from Col. Miller proceeding on leave	
		PM	Routine. Go to Calais and D.A.D.V.S.	
	10/8/18	AM	Routine.	

WAR DIARY
or
INTELLIGENCE SUMMARY.
(Erase heading not required.)

Army Form C. 2118.

Place	Date	Hour	Summary of Events and Information	Remarks and references to Appendices
Sheet 2.7 P34.0.1.2	11/8/15	10am	Routine	
		pm	attend commemoration Service at TERDIGHEM. HQrs. L. Vey present	
		pm	Church Parade for all ranks	
	12/8/15	am	Routine	
		pm	Visit all units under vety charge.	
	13/8/15	am pm	Routine	
			FSVS mob. inspection	
	14/8/15	am pm	Routine unravel 7 Sec arrived to Corps VS	
	15/8/15	am pm	Routine attend Conference FSVS Spec	
	16/8/15	am pm	Routine. HQ. QG inspect section	
	17/8/15	am pm	Routine. Visit all units.	
	18/8/15	am pm	Routine. Evacuate 11 Sick animals to Corps VS	
	19/8/15	am pm	Routine. HQ. L.C. inspect section	
	20/8/15	am pm	Routine. Present to Brehm & reconcile to MSCC. H. & S.	
	21/8/15	10am am	Routine. Visit all units under vety charge. Uhel Sick ls called Clyppy. Sick. Branch band & x 6 7 p. O.S.	
	22/8/15	10am am	Routine. attend Conference FSVS Office. FSVS hors. inspects section	
	23/8/15	am am	Routine	
	24/8/15	10am am pm	Routine Visit all units. attend 8 Corps horse show	
	25/8/15	10am pm	Routine. Visit all units. attend Church Parade	

Army Form C. 2118.

WAR DIARY
or
INTELLIGENCE SUMMARY.
(Erase heading not required.)

Instructions regarding War Diaries and Intelligence Summaries are contained in F. S. Regs., Part II. and the Staff Manual respectively. Title pages will be prepared in manuscript.

Place	Date	Hour	Summary of Events and Information	Remarks and references to Appendices
P.34.D.1.2.	26/8/18	10 m.Pm	Routine. Pay man had 31 Bn. Horse Show	
	27/8/18	10 m.Am	Routine. Vsd all units. Jump at Eluvenchy Ctrkd 10 Corps	
	28/8/18	10 m.Pm	Routine. Vsd Bn.s - HQ2s	
	29/8/18	m.A	Routine. Attend Conference 8 am 9 the	
	30/8/18	m.A	Routine. Wrote notes to 6 personel to England at large 6 Egypta orc	
	31/8/18	m.A	Routine. In attendance on V.O. & Corps Horse Show	

4 48 Mob Vety Sec 36
See

Army Form C. 2118.

Section Overseas,
5-10-15
Mobilized 20-8-15

WAR DIARY
or
INTELLIGENCE SUMMARY.
(Erase heading not required.)

Place	Date	Hour	Summary of Events and Information	Remarks and references to Appendices
P34.d.15 Sheet 24.	1/9/18	A.M.	Routine	Capt. Chown O.C. 48 MVS proceeds on 10 days leave prior to going to Egyptian Army.	
—		P.M.	Routine	Major Horne DADVS 36 Div takes over MVS @ Capt Chowns Vety charge.	
ditto	2/9/18	A.M.	Routine	Established an advance Vety Aid Post at R 35 A 3.0 Sheet 27.	
		P.M.	Routine		
ditto	3/9/18	A.M.		MVS move from P34 D.1.5 to R 28 D.8.9 Sheet 27 Vety Aid Post is withdrawn	
		P.M.		Installed M.V.S. & generally plan out the Farm.	
R18b89 Sheet 27.	4/9/18	A.M.	Routine	Visit No 2 Coy A.S.C. Div H.Q. 36 Signals	
		P.M.	Routine	DDVS II Army DADVS X Corps called. Inspects Section.	
"	5/9/18	A.M.		Evacuate 7 cases to X Corps V.E.S. (2 Artillery Saddler cases) Routine	
	6/9/18	A.M. P.M.	Routine Routine		
	7/9/18	A.M. P.M.	Routine Routine		
	8/9/18	A.M. P.M.	Routine Routine	My DADVS X Corps visits section. Fitzpatrick Cpl & Turner Pte on leave 8/9/18	
	9/9/18	A.M. P.M.	45 Remounts received	Unexpected Evacuate 14 animals to X Corps V.E.S.	
	10/9/18	A.M. P.M.	45 Remounts issued Routine		
	11/9/18	A.M. P.M.	Routine Routine		
	12/9/18	A.M. P.M.	Routine Evacuate	12 animals to X Corps V.E.S. Routine	

Army Form C. 2118.

WAR DIARY
or
INTELLIGENCE SUMMARY.

(Erase heading not required.)

Instructions regarding War Diaries and Intelligence Summaries are contained in F. S. Regs., Part II. and the Staff Manual respectively. Title pages will be prepared in manuscript.

Place	Date	Hour	Summary of Events and Information	Remarks and references to Appendices
	Sept 13	am pm	Routine. Pay out men.	
	14	am pm	Routine	
	15	am pm	Routine	
	16	am pm	Routine	
	17	am pm	Open new Imprest Account with X Corps.	
	18	am pm	Order Section to move on 19th inst.	
	19	am pm	M.V.S. moves to 27/P30 B.1.3.	
Roquettry.	20	am pm	M.V.S. moves to 27/C.1 D.7.2.	
"	21	am pm	Capt Stevens A.V.C. reports as new C.O. vice Capt H Cressor. Take him to Section Head him to take over.	
"	22	am pm	Capt Stevens A.V.C. takes over command of 48 M.V.S.	

Army Form C. 2118.

WAR DIARY
or
INTELLIGENCE SUMMARY.
(Erase heading not required.)

Instructions regarding War Diaries and Intelligence Summaries are contained in F. S. Regs., Part II. and the Staff Manual respectively. Title pages will be prepared in manuscript.

Place	Date	Hour	Summary of Events and Information	Remarks and references to Appendices
ESQUELBECQ	23	am	Routine taken command of H8 M.V.S. — Inspected stores of section as in AF G1098-89. Find same complete. 7 manstock owing to 6 being on leave & 1 evacuated sick.	
do	24	am	Routine.	
do	25	am	Routine.	
do	26	am	Routine.	
do	27	am	2 Horses evacuated to 8 VES. Section moves to F13 c 3.9. Sheet 28.	
	28	pm	Section moved to H.2.c.6.6.8. Sheet 28.	
	29	pm	Section moved to H.6.c.4.2. Sheet 28.	
	30		Routine.	

48 Mob. V.S. U.S.

M.V.S. Hatyia 28/9/15
arrival ovxiii 5/10/15

WAR DIARY
or
INTELLIGENCE SUMMARY.

Army Form C. 2118.

(Erase heading not required.)

Place	Date	Hour	Summary of Events and Information	Remarks and references to Appendices
Hatyia	Oct 1		Arrivals Evac to 2 YES (base)	
Mudros	" 2		Established. Advances (50) of J. K & Y E (Shed 28)	
Roylin	" 3		Docks aid Pol. 11 Evac? to 30 MVS	
"	" 4		Info. R.T.O. Chickfield to A.P. O sec?	
Cahit	" 5		Hosp Equipmts No Established 30 ft Lot. 10 kSignal	
Roylin	" 6		Sent Stockland rake A.P.	
Roylin	" 7		Visited aid Pol	
Roylin	" 8		Supplies sent as Pot.	
Roylin	" 9		30 Rthounds Received t dukhl. 1 shot. Frates aid pol.	
Roylin	" 10		Conference at HQ	
Roylin	" 11		Visit to aid pol	
Roylin	" 13		5 Evac? to 130 MVS Rahara sen? leave 8 evac. Pass out 8 hors	
Roylin	" 15		4 Evac? to 30 MVS	
	" 14		Section moved to C.30 ended Sech 28. Evac? 21 to 30 VES	
	" 15		Section moved to J.17 a.a.o. Steel 28. " " No 30 MVS	
	" 16		Section moved to K.7926 " Y k.o.	

H.N. Turner A/Lieut

Army Form C. 2118.

WAR DIARY
or
INTELLIGENCE SUMMARY.
(Erase heading not required.)

Instructions regarding War Diaries and Intelligence Summaries are contained in F. S. Regs., Part II. and the Staff Manual respectively. Title pages will be prepared in manuscript.

D.A.D.V.S.
36th
ULSTER DIVISION
No. _____
Date _____

Place	Date	Hour	Summary of Events and Information	Remarks and references to Appendices
	Oct 17		Section moved to L.1 cent: 8 Horses evac'd to 50 MVS.	
	" 18		Routine.	
	" 19		Section moves to A.22.C.8.8. Shed 29. 1 Heat case to 2 YES.	
	" 20		Routine	
	" 21		Routine.	
	" 22		Routine. Sergt. Strickland returned to No 12 Y.H.	
	" 23		Routine.	
	" 24		Moves Section to B.21.d.7.5. Shed 29. Evac'd 5 horse to 50 MVS	
	" 25		Routine.	
	" 26		Routine.	
	" 27		Routine. Received & distributed 50 Panjanks. 5 Animals evac'd 50 MVS	
LAEIWE	" 28		Routine. Evac to 50 MVS. Sergt Crew reported for duty.	
	" 29		Moves MVS to LAEIWE	
	" 30		Routine. 10 Animals " " YES.	
	" 31		Routine. 21 " " " "	

WAR DIARY
or
INTELLIGENCE SUMMARY

Army Form C. 2118.

4.8 Mobile Vety Sec E.A.F.

Embarked for Overseas 5.10.15

Place	Date	Hour	Summary of Events and Information	Remarks and references to Appendices
STERHOEK	Nov 1	Routine	6 Evac. 10 Y YES.	
	2	Routine	8 " 5 5 animals (STERHOEK).	
	3	Surplus kit sent to Ordnance. Tents + other equipmt sent to ordnance store.		
	4	Routine	14 animals 16 10 YES.	
	5	Routine		
	6	Routine	8 " 10 YES	
	7	Routine	Remounts Arrhelo Stores moved, mules gone	
	8	Routine		
	9	Routine	4 " Received 47 animals to animal	
	10	Routine	5 HQ Horses, shipping	
	11	Routine	60	
	12	Routine	60	
	13	Routine	60	
	14	Routine	60	
	15	Routine	3 animals to 10 V.S.	
	16	Routine	25 Horses despatched to 9th VS.	
	17	Routine	5 Animals to 10 V.S. HQ Signals, shipping	
	18	Routine	60	
	19	Routine	60	
	20	Routine	60	
	21	Routine		
	22	Routine		
	23	Routine		
	24	Routine		
	25	Routine		
	26	Routine		
	27	Routine		
	28	Routine		
	29	Routine		
	30	Routine	60 60 60 60	

W.S.Thrum
Capt. A.V.C.

Army Form C. 2118.

WAR DIARY
or
INTELLIGENCE SUMMARY.
(Erase heading not required.)

48 MVS

Place	Date	Hour	Summary of Events and Information	Remarks and references to Appendices
STEENWERK	1		Routine	
	2		"	
MOUSERON	3		Moved Section to Mouscron	
	4		Routine	
	5		Routine	
	6		Evacuated 9 animals to 15 V.E.S.	
	7		"	
	8		Evacuated 3 animals to 15 V.E.S.	
	9			
	10		ROUTINE.	
	11		Evacuated 4 animals to 15 V.E.S.	
	12		"	
	13		"	
	14		"	
	15		Evac. 4 animals to 15 V.E.S.	
	16		"	
	17		"	
	18		Evac. 10 animals to 15 V.E.S.	
	19		"	
	20		Evac. 16 animals to 15 V.E.S.	
	21		"	
	22		Evac. 6 animals to V.E.S. 13th	
	23		"	
	24		Evac. 1 animal to V.E.S. 15th	
	25		"	
	26		"	
	27		Evac. 6 animals to 15th V.E.S.	

WAR DIARY
or
INTELLIGENCE SUMMARY.

(Erase heading not required.)

Army Form C. 2118.

D.A.D.V.S.
36TH
(ULSTER DIVISION).
No. VD 2461
Date 31/1/19

M.V.T. Mobilised 6.10.15
M.V.T. Mobilised 20.8.15

Place	Date 1919	Hour	Summary of Events and Information	Remarks and references to Appendices
Mouscron	Jan 1	Routine	Evacuate 16 Horses to 15.Y.E.S.	
"	2	"		
"	3	"	Evacuate 1 Horse to 15 Y.E.S.	
"	4	"	Evacuate 2 horses to 15 Y.E.S.	
"	5	"	Evacuate 4 horses & 1 Mule to 15 Y.E.S.	
"	6	"		
"	7	"	Evacuate 1 Horse and 2 Mules to 15 Y.E.S.	
"	8	"	Evacuate 3 Horses & 2 Mules to 15 Y.E.S.	
"	9	"		
"	10	"	1 Horse of 16 R.I.R. Sold to Theophile Rouse, Mouscron	
"	11	"		
"	12	"		
"	13	"	Evacuate 2 Horses & 2 Mules to 15 Y.E.S.	
"	14	"		
"	15	"	Evacuate 3 Horses to 15 Y.E.S.	
"	16	"	Evacuate 1 Mule to 15 Y.E.S.	
"	17	"		
"	18	"		
"	19	"	Evacuate 5 Horses & 2 Mules to 15 Y.E.S.	
"	20	"		
"	21	"	Evacuate 6 Horses & 3 Mules to 15 Y.E.S.	
"	22	"		
"	23	"	Evacuate 3 Horses & 1 Mule to 15 Y.E.S.	
"	24	"		
"	25	"		
"	26	"		
"	27	"	Evacuate 3 Horses to 15 Y.E.S.	
"	28	"	Board Animals.	
"	29	"		
"	30	"		
"	31	"		

Capt ANC

WAR DIARY
or
INTELLIGENCE SUMMARY.

Army Form C. 2118.

45. M.V.S.
Mobilised 20.8.15
Embarked for Rouen 5.10.15.

D.A.D.V.S.
36TH
(ULSTER) DIVISION.
No VD 2582
Date 1.3.19

Place	Date	Hour	Summary of Events and Information	Remarks and references to Appendices
MOUSCRON	Feb.1919 1		Routine. Evacuate 5 animals to 15.V.E.S.	
do	2		do " 4 "	
do	3		do " 5 "	
do	4		do " " "	
do	5		do " 2 "	
do	6		do " 4 "	
do	7		do " 3 "	
do	8		do " 7 "	
do	9		do " " "	
do	10		do " " "	Granted 14 days leave to U.K.
do	11		do " " "	
do	12		do " " "	
do	13		do " 9 "	
do	14		do " 4 "	
do	15		do " 3 "	
do	16		do " " "	
do	17		do " " "	
do	18		do " " "	
do	19		do " 2 "	
do	20		do " 3 "	
do	21		do " 1 "	
do	22		do " " "	
do	23		do " " "	
do	24		do " " "	
do	25		do " " "	
do	26		do " " "	
do	27		do " " "	
do	28		do " " "	Returned from leave 14 days.

Army Form C. 2118.
36TH (ULSTER) DIVISION
No WD 29/12

WAR DIARY
or
INTELLIGENCE SUMMARY.
(Erase heading not required.)

Place	Date	Hour	Summary of Events and Information	Remarks and references to Appendices
Mouscron	April 1919 1		Routine	
Do	2		"	
Do	3		" Evacuated 4 animals to 15 V.E.S. Despatch 8 Riders to Linselles Camp.	
Do	4		"	
Do	5		" Despatch 1 Corpl. to 6 M.V.S. 1 Cpl. to 15 V.E.S. Evacuate 4 animals to 15 V.E.S	
Do	6		" Sgt Scholfield, Ptes Turner & Fletcher proceed to Concentration Camp for Demobilisation	
Do	7		" Routine	
Do	8		" Do	
Do	9		" Routine	
Do	10		" Evacuate 1 animal to 15 V.E.S.	
Do	11		" Evacd 1 animal to 15 V.E.S	
Do	12		" Routine	
Do	13		" Did Ration returns on leave Ireland	
Do	14		" Routine	
Do	15		" Routine	
Do	16		" Received 1 Mule from 280th (Railway) Company R.E. Loining Surplus;	
Do	17		" Evacuated 1 Mule to 15 V.E.S. (Completed 280 Railway Co. R.E. Central Surplus animals)	
Do	18		" Routine	
Do	19		" Evacuated 1 animal to 15 V.E.S	
Do	20		" Routine	
Do	21		" 15/5 Cl Pte joined from 108 Hospital Dieppe	
Do	22		" Routine	
Do	23		" 2Cl Pte joined from 11 Encr M.V.S. 66 Div	
Do	24		"	
Do	25		" Evacuated 2 Horses to 15 V.E.S	

J.G. Miller Capt RAVC

Army Form C. 2118.

WAR DIARY
or
INTELLIGENCE SUMMARY.

(Erase heading not required.)

Place	Date	Hour	Summary of Events and Information	Remarks and references to Appendices
April 1919	26		Routine	
	27		Routine	
	28		Routine	
	29		1 Sgt & 1 Private joined from M.V. Rouen	
	30		Routine	

J.C. Miller Captain
A.V.C.

30/4/19

Army Form C. 2118.

WAR DIARY
or
INTELLIGENCE SUMMARY.
(Erase heading not required.)

Place	Date	Hour	Summary of Events and Information	Remarks and references to Appendices
Lille	October 10th		Return from Hospital and take over duties of Senior Veterinary Officer No 5 District from Major R.A. Plunkett R.A.V.C. Authority D.D.V.S. letter dated 23/9/19. No 3/5/19.	
	11th		Ote Mouight, R.A. admitted to Hospital. Visit units in No 5 Labour Group for inspection	
	12th		Visits 4th Army Auxe Horse Coy and 99th Infantry Brigade H.Q. an Chaise to inspect animals	
	13th		Routine. Horses and Mules for sale at Lille Madeleine	
	14th		Visit 113 Chinese Labour Coy and HQ. No 5 Labour Group for inspection of animals. Routine work at 48 M.V.S.	
	15th		Sale of animals at Lille. 34 animals sold and go to Chehin to join in proceeds of sale. Routine work at 48 M.V.S.	

WAR DIARY or INTELLIGENCE SUMMARY

Army Form C. 2118.

Place	Date	Hour	Summary of Events and Information	Remarks and references to Appendices
	16th		Visit to POPERINGHE to see Capt R.R. Williamson R.A.V.C. and Routine work at 4 M.V.C. to inspect animals.	
	17th		Routine :- 32 Animals received from No 4 Veterinary Hospital CALAIS for No 5 Mills Horse Butcher 14½E weighed & disposed of	
	18th		Routine :- Visit Cachin to pay proceeds of Animals sold to No Mills, H.F.M.V.C. Proceeded to Tournai Petit Enghien to inspect animals 50 & Labour Group.	
	19th		Visit POPERINGHE with Mo Mills to inspect arrangements for receiving animals for Butchery at abeel.	
	20th		Visit H.Q. No 5 Labour Group to attend dog with Broken leg. Proceeded to Tournai. Emergency animal of No 50 Labour Group. 24 Animals received from No 4 Veterinary Hospital CALAIS weighed.	

Army Form C. 2118.

WAR DIARY
or
INTELLIGENCE SUMMARY.
(Erase heading not required.)

Place	Date	Hour	Summary of Events and Information	Remarks and references to Appendices
	21st		Routine:- Visit No 80 Labour Group at TOURNAI to inspect Animals. One Sergeant, one Corporal & 10 Men arrive to replace Men eligible for Demobilization	
	22nd		Routine:- Men eligible for demobilization sent to No 4 Veterinary Hospital. Visit POPERINGHE to inspect Animals also, in Conference with D.A.D.R. at No 5 Area Animal Collecting Camp at ARQUES.	
	23rd		Visit No 6 Labour Coy at MERVILLE to see an injured Mule. Proceeds to Rephinghe to arrange for graduates of M.V.S.	
	24th		D.D.V.S. visits Unit in unsuspected duty. 64 Animals received from No 4 Veterinary Hospital Calais for No 1 Mule Horse Butchery. Weighed Motor Ambulance collects injured Mule from No 6 Labour Coy MERVILLE & Animals D.D & L & No. 5 Area Animal Collecting Camp for Butchery.	

Army Form C. 2118.

WAR DIARY
or
INTELLIGENCE SUMMARY.
(Erase heading not required.)

Instructions regarding War Diaries and Intelligence Summaries are contained in F. S. Regs., Part II. and the Staff Manual respectively. Title pages will be prepared in manuscript.

Place	Date	Hour	Summary of Events and Information	Remarks and references to Appendices
	25th		Routine:- Visit 19th Army Horse Show - day to inspect Animals	
	26th		Routine:- Inspect Animal with Units in No 5 Labour Group	
	27th		Routine:- 13 Animals weighed and over to Mr Mills Horse Butcher LILLE. Rentes work at 45. M.V.S.	
	28th		Routine:- 138 Animals received from 44th Mo V.S. for Mr Mills Horse Butcher LILLE:- 40 weighed & disposed of.	
	29th		Routine:- 40 Animal weighed for Mr Mill. Visit TOURNAI to inspect Animals in No 80 Labour Group	
	30th		Remaining 58 Animals weighed for Mr Mills. 2 Animals received from 40 Veterinary Hospital Orders for Mr Mills. Routine work at 45 M.V.S.	

Army Form C. 2118.

WAR DIARY
or
INTELLIGENCE SUMMARY.
(Erase heading not required.)

Army HVS November 1919

Place	Date	Hour	Summary of Events and Information	Remarks and references to Appendices
	31st		Routine:- Visit 98th Infantry Bdge to inspect Animal. Also 7th Army Aux Horse Coy	
	November 1st		Routine:- Motor Ambulance goes to 12th Army Aux Horse Coy at POTIJZE to collect 2 sick animals. Collect and pay to Orderlies money for Animals sold to Mr Mills	
	2nd		Routine:- Visit to POPERINGHE and see Capt. D.R. Williams R.A.V.C. i/c more 2 R.E.M.V.S. Also Visit D.A.D.R at No 5 Animal Collecting Camp	
	3rd		Routine:- Visit units in No 5 Labour Group	
	4th		Routine:- Motor Ambulance goes to VLAMERTINGHE to Collect Horse & Animals Tieued from No 4 Veterinary Hospital Calais for Mr Mills	

Place	Date	Hour	Summary of Events and Information	Remarks and references to Appendices
	5th		Routine:- Visit to POPERINGHE and VLAMERTINGHE to select Billets and stables for the Unit	
	6th		Routine:- 9 Animals sold to Butcher. Visit to No 5 Area Animal Collecting Camp at ARQUES Received from 2/01 Labour Coy for Butchery 7 Animals	
	7th		Routine:- Packing Stores ready to move 45 M.V.C. Vlamertinghe	
	8th		Routine:- Horse Transport proceeds to new Billets at Hospital Farm Camp near VLAMERTINGHE Visit Cashier to pay money for Animals sold to Butcher	

WAR DIARY
or
INTELLIGENCE SUMMARY.
(Erase heading not required.)

Army Form C. 2118.

Place	Date	Hour	Summary of Events and Information	Remarks and references to Appendices
	9th		Section moves to Aispiete Farm Camp near VLAMERTINGHE	
	10th		Handover duties of St Senior Veterinary Officer, and no pistol Command of 18th Mobile Veterinary Section to Capt. R. R. Williamson R.A.V.C., prior to proceeding to U.K. for duty. Authority D.D.V.S. letter no 4/5363/19 dated 31/10/19	

W.H.Thomas
Capt. R.A.V.C.

www.ingramcontent.com/pod-product-compliance
Lightning Source LLC
Chambersburg PA
CBHW081534160426
43191CB00011B/1760